DRUG I.D. & SYMPTOM GUIDE

4th Edition

QWIK-CODE

LawTech Publishing

QWIK-CODE is a trademark of *LawTech Publishing Co., Ltd*.

LawTech Publishing Co., Ltd.

1.800.498.0911
info@lawtechpublishing.com
www.lawtechpublishing.com

Comments and suggestions are welcome.

Contributing Editor: Trinka Porrata, President, Project GHB

pp. 224

v.03.23.09

Printed in China

ISBN: 978-1-56325-097-2

TABLE OF CONTENTS

DISSOCIATIVE ANESTHETICS

STIMULANTS

PARAPHERNALIA

NEEDLE INJECTIONS

APPENDIX

CANNABIS

MARIJUANA

(Cannabis)

Dried Marijuana

Marijuana Leaf

MARIJUANA

Visual Description:
A dried, green leafy substance mixed with stems and possibly seeds.

Methods of Use:
Ingested, Smoked

Effects:
Onset – 8-10 Seconds
Peak – 10-30 Minutes
Duration – 6-8 Hours

Symptoms of Use:
Nystagmus – No
Pupils – Normal (Possibly Dilated)
Pulse – Elevated
Blood Pressure – Elevated
Body Temperature – Near Normal
Non-Convergence – Yes

Bloodshot Eyes
Body Tremors
Debris in Mouth
Difficulty Concentrating
Disoriented
Eyelid Tremors
Impaired Divided Attention
Impaired Time/Distance Perception
Increased Appetite
Odor of Burning Marijuana
Rebound Dilation
Relaxed Inhibitions

Overdose Symptoms:
Fatigue
Paranoia
Psychosis

MARIJUANA CIGARETTE/THAI STICK

Thai Sticks

Packaged Marijuana and Marijuana Cigarettes

MARIJUANA CIGARETTE/THAI STICK

Visual Description:
A dried, green leafy substance mixed with stems and possibly seeds, hand-rolled into a cigarette (joint).

Methods of Use:
Smoked

Duration of Effects:
Onset – 8-10 Seconds
Peak – 10-30 Minutes
Duration – Variable

Symptoms of Use:
Nystagmus – No
Pupils – Normal (Possibly Dilated)
Pulse – Elevated
Blood Pressure – Elevated
Body Temperature – Near Normal
Non-Convergence – Yes

Bloodshot Eyes
Body Tremors
Debris in Mouth
Difficulty Concentrating
Disoriented
Eyelid Tremors
Impaired Divided Attention
Impaired Time/Distance Perception
Increased Appetite
Odor of Burning Marijuana
Rebound Dilation
Relaxed Inhibitions

Overdose Symptoms:
Fatigue
Paranoia
Psychosis

MARIJUANA GROW

Marijuana "Grow"

Marijuana "Grow" showing
individual potted plants.

MARIJUANA GROW

To establish evidence for a cultivation charge:

- Photographically document the roots of plants to demonstrate live plant status at time of seizure.
- Document/seize evidence such as weighing devices and articles showing identity of persons in control of premises.
- Outdoor cultivation – pipes (buried or above ground), hoses or other evidence of irrigation systems consistent with marijuana cultivation; other trees, shrubs or plants planted or maintained to hide marijuana plants from view; gardening tools, fertilizer, seeds, sheds/facilities for hanging, drying, processing and packaging for distribution; security devices or systems such as video surveillance, booby traps and armed security personnel.
- Indoor cultivation – grow lights, tubing or hoses or pipes arranged for use as an irrigation system for watering individual plants or maintaining a hydroponic garden; seeds, plant medium, various sizes of pots, foil to cover walls and/or ceilings to reflect light and heat inward (improving growth patterns and/or limiting heat escape); transformers, heating/cooling and lighting systems for cultivation; security systems; facilities for hanging, drying, processing, storing, packaging and mailing of marijuana.
- Also: literature, magazines and computer data regarding cultivation techniques, especially those specific to marijuana; pays and owes regarding distribution of narcotics.
- Computer equipment or electronic storage devices, handwritten notes or printed confidential password lists to enter secured files; indicators of Internet usage and "favorite" or "bookmarked" Internet locations dealing with the use, cultivation and trafficking of marijuana and other narcotics.

Medical Marijuana

The status of "medical marijuana" varies from state-to-state as to quantities allowed to grow for "Personal Use" and other conditions of use.

HASHISH OIL

Hash Oil (Dark)

Hash Oil

HASHISH OIL

Visual Description:
Concentrated, thick liquid, dark or gold in color.

Methods of Use:
Smoked - Mixed with tobacco or marijuana.

Effects:
Onset – 8-10 Seconds
Peak – 10-30 Minutes
Duration – 4-6 Hours (variable)

Symptoms:
Nystagmus – No
Pupils – Normal (Possibly Dilated)
Pulse – Elevated Blood
Pressure – Elevated
Body Temperature – Near Normal
Non-Convergence – Yes

Bloodshot Eyes
Body Tremors
Debris in Mouth
Difficulty Concentrating
Disoriented
Eyelid Tremors
Impaired Divided Attention
Impaired Time/Distance Perception
Increased Appetite
Odor of Burning Marijuana
Rebound Dilation
Relaxed Inhibitions

Overdose Symptoms:
Fatigue
Paranoia
Psychosis

HASHISH

Hashish in bag used for transportation.

Hashish and bag shown with 10 cent coin
for comparison.

HASHISH

Visual Description:
Solid dark green or gold substance.

Methods of Use:
Ingested, Smoked

Effects:
Onset – 8-10 Seconds
Peak – 10-30 Minutes
Duration – 4-6 Hours (variable)

Symptoms:
Nystagmus – No
Pupils – Normal (Possibly Dilated)
Pulse – Elevated Blood Pressure
Body Temperature - Near Normal
Non-Convergence – Yes

Bloodshot Eyes
Body Tremors
Debris in Mouth
Difficulty Concentrating
Disoriented
Eyelid Tremors
Impaired Divided Attention
Impaired Time/Distance Perception
Increased Appetite
Odor of Burning Marijuana
Rebound Dilation
Relaxed Inhibitions

Overdose Symptoms:
Fatigue
Paranoia
Psychosis

This page intentionally left blank.

DEPRESSANTS

ALCOHOL (ETHANOL)

Visual Description:
Liquid, various odors, colors & flavors. Also found in some perfumes, after-shaves, food flavorings (i.e. vanilla, almond, lemon extracts).

Effects:
Onset – Rapid (varies with quantity consumed and rate of consumption)
Duration – Roughly .02 BAC metabolized per hour.

Method of Use:
Ingested. Some reports of alcohol enemas in college scene.

Symptoms:
Nystagmus – Yes
Pupils – Near normal size, reaction slowed
Pulse – Elevated
Blood Pressure – Elevated
Body Temperature – Subnormal
Non-Convergence – Yes

Euphoria
Lack of Coordination
Slurred Speech
Exaggerated Emotional State
Reduced Visual Acuity, Peripheral Vision & Glare Recovery
Ataxia
Impaired Judgment & Reflexes
Increased Pain Threshold
Reduced Inhibitions
Boisterous or Aggressive Behavior

Overdose Symptoms:
Incontinence
Inability to Stand or Walk
Coma
Respiratory Depression
Pulmonary Aspiration
Death

ALCOHOL

Delirium Tremens (DTs)

May begin within 48-72 hours for chronic heavy abusers who stop their consumption of alcohol.

NOTE:

The average adult can metabolize about 7-10 g of alcohol per hour (rate variable per individual and overall blood alcohol level). While tolerance may vary greatly in individuals, generally speaking an ethanol level below 300 mg/dL in a comatose patient presented to the ER will initiate a search for alternative causes (medical condition or other drugs).

Body Fluids Required For Testing:

While breath and blood are the preferred samples for alcohol alone, urine should be considered if other drugs are suspected.

BARBITURATES

Miscellaneous Barbiturate Capsules

Miscellaneous Barbiturate Tablets

BARBITURATES

Drug Name – Trade Name (representative)
   Amobarbital – Amytal
   Butalbital – Fiorinal or Fioricet
   Mephobarbital – Mebaral
   Pentobarbital – Numbutal
   Phenobarbital – Luminal
   Secobarbital – Seconal, Tuinal
   Butabarbital Sodium – Butisol
   Methohexital – Brevital
   Thiopental – Pentothal

Visual Description:
   Various colored capsules. Most commonly abused are secobarbital (red devils), pentobarbital (yellow jackets) and amobarbital (blue angles).

Methods of Use:
   Ingested, injected, snorted

Duration of Effects:
   1-16 hours depending on which drug taken.

Possible Effects:
   Sedation, Hypnosis and/or Deep coma
   Anesthesia
   Lethargy
   Slurred speech
   Nystagmus
   Ataxia
   Mild to Severe Intoxication

   Barbiturates range from ultra short acting, such as methohexital and thiopental; to short acting, such as pentobarbital; to intermediate acting, such as amobarbital or butabarbital; to long acting, such as phenobarbital or methobarbital. Typically used as hypnotic/sedative agents, for induction of anesthesia, treatment of epilepsy, and as anticonvulsants.

Special testing notes:
   Short/intermediate acting barbiturates may be detected in urine 24-72 hours; longer acting barbiturates up to seven days.

17

NON-BARBITURATES

Soma [front]

Soma [back]

NON-BARBITURATES

Drug Name – Trade Name (representative)
- **Buspirone** – BuSpar
- **Carisoprodol** — Soma
- **Chloral hydrate** – Noctec, Somnote, Aquachloral, Supprettes
- **Ethchlorvynol** – Placidyl
- **Ethinamate** – (no US or Canada brand)
- **Glutethimide** – Doriden
- **Meprobamate** – Miltown, Equanil
- **Methaqualone** – Quaalude
- **Methocarbamol** – Robaxin
- **Methyprylon** – Moludar
- **Paraldehyde** – Paral

Visual Description:
Various colors and brands of tablets.

Methods of Use:
Ingested, injected, snorted

Duration of Effects:
1-16 hours depending on which drug taken.

Possible Effects:
Sedation, Hypnosis and/or Deep coma
Anesthesia
Lethargy
Slurred Speech
Nystagmus
Ataxia
Mild to Severe Intoxication

NOTE:
Methaqualone pharmaceutical products were discontinued in 1984 in US. May see counterfeit, foreign or old stock.

ANTI-PSYCHOTIC TRANQUILIZERS

Haloperidol (Haldol)

Lithium (Eskalith)

ANTI-PSYCHOTIC TRANQUILIZERS

Drug Name – Trade Name (representative)
- **Chlorpromazine** – Thorazine
- **Clozapine** – Clozaril
- **Droperidol** – Inapsine
- **Fluphenazine HCl** – Prolixin
- **Haloperidol** – Haldol
- **Lithium** – Eskalith, Lithobid, Lithane (Canada)
- **Loxapine** – Loxitane
- **Mesoridazine** – Serentil
- **Molindone** – Moban
- **Olanzapine** – Zyprexa
- **Perphenazine** – Trilafon
- **Prochlorperazine** – Compazine
- **Promethazine** – Phenergan
- **Risperidone** – Risperdal
- **Seroquel** – Quetiapine Fumarate
- **Thioridazine** – Mellaril
- **Trimethobenzamide** – Tigan

Visual Description:
Various Tablets

Methods of Use:
Ingested, Snorted

Possible Symptoms:
Mild to severe intoxication, sedation, dry mouth (Exception: Clozapine Can cause hypersalivation)
Absence of sweating
Tachycardia
Coma
Seizures
Jaw Muscle Spasm
Rigidity
Respiratory Arrest.
Either hypothermia or hyperthermia may be seen.
Overdose may be seen in suicide attempts though some are not extremely toxic.

ANTI-DEPRESSANTS

Trazadone (Desyrel)

Prozac

ANTI-DEPRESSANTS

Drug Name – Trade Name (representative)
Amitriptyline HCl – Elavil
Amoxapine – Asendin
Bupropion – Wellbutrin, Zyban
Citalopram HCl – Celexa
Clomipramine – Anafranil
Desipramine – Norpramine
Doxepin HCl – Sinequan
Escitalopram – Lexapro
Fluoxetine – Prozac
Fluvoxamine – Luvox
Imipramine – Rofranil
Isocarboxazide – Marplan
Maprotiline – Ludiomil
Mirtazapine – Remeron
Nefazodone – Serzone
Nortriptyline – Aventyl or Pamelor
Paroxetine – Paxil
Phenelzine – Nardil
Protryptaline – Vivactil, Triptil (Canada)
Sertraline HCl – Zoloft
Tranylcypromine – Pamate
Trazadone – Desyrel
Trimipramine – Surmontil, Apo-Trimip (Canada)
Venlafaxine – Effexor

Visual Description:
Various

Methods of Use:
Ingested, Injected, Snorted

Possible Effects:
Overdose may cause ataxia, sedation, seizures, coma. Can produce restlessness, anxiety and agitation, especially Bupropion. Mirtazapine (Remeron) has a prominent sedative effect.

NOTES:
Noncyclic anti-depressants such as Desyrel, Serzone, Prozac, Zoloft, Paxil, Luvox, Effexor and Wellbutrin, are typically less toxic than the tricyclics, such as Elavil, Asendin, Anafranil, Sinequan, Rofranil, Ludiomil, Aventyl, etc. Tricyclics are sometimes used in suicidal overdoses and represent a significant cause of poisoning in hospitalizations and deaths.

These drugs are listed in the DEPRESSANTS category based on their overall action of depressing the body's central nervous system. The term "anti-depressants" refers to the action of the drugs in adjusting the user's mental mood. The FDA now requires most anti-depressant medications to warn that these drugs may increase risks of suicidal thinking and behavior.

BENZODIAZEPINES

Flunitrazepam (Rohypnol)

Lorazepam (Ativan)

Diazepam (Valium)

Clonazepam
(Klonopin or Rivotril - Mexico)

Xanax

BENZODIAZEPINES

Drug Name – Trade Name (representative)

Alprazolam – Xanax, Niravam
Bromazepam – Lexotan (Mexico)
Chlordiazepoxide – Librium
Clonazepam – Klonopin or Rivotril (Mexico)
Clorazepate – Tranzene
Diazepam – Valium
Estazolam – ProSom
Flunitrazepam – Rohypnol (aka roofies)

Flurazepam – Dalmane
Halazepam – Paxipam
Lorazepam – Ativan
Midazolam – Versed
Nitrazepam – Mogadan
Oxazepam – Serax
Prazepam – Centrax
Quazepam – Doral
Temazepam – Restoril
Triazolam – Halcion

Visual Description:
Various tablets; may be ground up for snorting. Used to dose others for rape or robbery; may be powder or dissolved into liquid (in small vial or nasal spray or eye drop container)

Methods of Use:
Ingested, Injected, Snorted

Possible Effects:
Benzodiazepine drugs give a wide range of typical CNS depressant effects. Typically used as anti-anxiety tranquilizers, sleep aids, withdrawal treatment for other drugs, seizure medications, etc. Causes sedation, blurred vision, drowsiness, lethargy, ataxia, fatigue, mental depression, loss of coordination, hypotension, diminished reflexes, confusion, coma, etc. Hypothermia possible.

Special Testing Note:
Some of these drugs are difficult to capture in testing. Some may not show up in a drug "screen" and require further testing. Triazolam and prazepam are particularly difficult to detect. Newer benzodiazepines or low concentrations may not be detected.

NOTE:
Flunitrazepam (Rohypnol) and bromazepam (Lexotan) are not approved for use in the United States but are commonly smuggled into the US for abuse purposes, especially from Mexico. Foreign prescriptions for flunitrazepam are not honored in the US.

GHB/XYREM/GBL/BD/OTHER ANALOGS

Miscellaneous forms of GBL.

GBL packaged as nail polish remover.

GHB Analogs

GBL "Super Glue Remover"

GHB "Mouthwash"

GHB "Somax"

GHB packaged as evidence.

GHB/XYREM/GBL/BD/OTHER ANALOGS
(Depressant/Dissociative Anesthetic)

Visual Description:
Commonly liquid, various textures; clear or yellowish color. Often colored for disguise or to avoid accidental consumption. No distinguishing odor – from mild chemical odor to nasty smell. Salty taste, but masked by sweet/fruity drinks. May see powder or capsules. Hydroscopic – likely to become moist if exposed to damp air.

Method of Use:
Ingested. Reported rectal insertion of GHB-soaked tampons, called "teabagging."

Duration of Effects:
Onset – 10-20 minutes (some analogs slightly slower)
Duration – 3-5 hours

Possible Symptoms:
Nystagmus – Vertical usually present (may be absent in low levels)
Pupils – Slow to react; near normal size
Pulse/Blood Pressure – generally lowered, may be high (not consistent)
Body Temperature – Near normal to low
Non-Convergence - Yes

Dizziness
Lack of Facial Expression (blank stare)
Droopy Eyelids (Ptosis)
Amnesia
Vomiting/Nausea
Aggression/Combativeness or Sexual Stimulation Possible
Drunken Behavior (without odor of alcohol)
Muscle Tone from Flaccid to Periods of Rigidity
Sudden Resolution of Symptoms (after approx 4 hours)

Overdose Symptoms:

Loss of Bowel and Urinary Control	Pulmonary Edema
Cold & Clammy Skin	Death
Coma	

Shallow Respiration (may drop to only 5-6 times per minute)

Special Testing Issues:
GHB is in blood 3-5 hours and urine approximately 12 hours

Associated Chemical/Analog Names
Gamma hydroxybutyrate (GHB); gamma butyrolactone (GBL); 1,4 butanediol (BD or BDO); pyrrolidone; gamma valerolactone (GVL); gamma hydroxyvalerate (GHV); octanediol; tetrahydrofuranone; tetramethylene glycol.

MISCELLANEOUS DEPRESSANTS

Sonata

Ambien 5 Mg

MISCELLANEOUS DEPRESSANTS

ANTIHISTAMINES
Diphenhydramine HCl – Benadryl
Hydroxyzine – Vistaral, Atarax, Pliva (Vet use)

SLEEPING MEDICATIONS
Eszopiclone — Lunesta
Zaleplon — Sonata
Zolpidem – Ambien

NOTE: While diphenhydramine is a common over-the-counter ingredient, it is impairing for purposes of driving and for use in drugging for robbery or rape, etc. Ambien has been identified in a number of drug rape cases and has been associated with "sleep driving" incidents of DUI and other sleep-walking incidents in which the person has no recall of the conduct.   Any drug that causes amnesia or unconsciousness or confusion could be utilized for robbery or rape.

This page intentionally left blank.

HALLUCINOGENS

PHENETHYLAMINES

"Mitsubishi" MDMA
(shown with penny for size comparison)

MDMA Fake
Actually Remifeminin, a harmless dietary
supplement that happens to have a butterfly
imprint and has been seen sold as Ecstasy. This
product has the butterfly on both sides, rare for an
actual MDMA pill.

MDMA with Calvin Klein "brand"

MDMA with Calvin Klein "brand"

MDMA "Budda"

MDMA "Green Clover"

MDMA User
(Note Extremely Dilated Pupils)

MDMA Capsules

PHENETHYLAMINES

2C-B — 4-bromo-2,5-dimethoxyphenethylamine
  (Bromo, Nexus)
2C-I — 2,5-dimethoxy-4-iodophenethylamine
2C-T-7 — 2,5-dimethoxy-4-(n)-propylthiophenethylamine
  (Lucky 7, Tripstacy)
2-TOM — 5-methoxy-4-methyl-2-methylthioamphetamine
3C-BZ — 4-benzyloxy-3,5-dimethoxyamphetamine
3C-E — 3,5-dimethoxy-4-ethoxyamphetamine
5-TOM — 2-methoxy-4-methyl-5-methylthio-A
MDMA — 3,4 methylenedioxy-methamphetamine
  (See MDMA, Ecstasy page)
MDA — 3,4 methylenedioxy-amphetamine

NOTE: There are at least 179 drugs in the category. 2C-B and 2C-I are the most common, after MDMA and MDA. But there are others such as: **2C-C, 2C-D, 2C-E, 2C-G, 2C-G-5, 2C-N, 2C-P, 2C-T, 2C-T-2, 2C-T-4, 2C-T-5, 2C-T-8, 2C-T-9, 3C-BZ, 2-4-DMA, DOM, HOT-2, 4-MA, MDDM, MDBZ, MDMC, MEDA, MMDA, 4-TIM, TMA-4, 4-T-TRIS**

Visual Description:
  Powder or pills, various colors and shapes; with or without logo imprints

Methods of Use:
  Ingested primarily as pills. May be snorted, injected or inserted rectally

Duration of Effects:
  Varies greatly with the substance taken

Possible Effects:
  Pupils – Dilated   **Pulse** – Elevated
  Blood Pressure – Elevated **Body Temperature** – Elevated
These drugs are generally hallucinogenic stimulants but with varying effects. Some are more hallucinogenic and some are more stimulant oriented. The effects will be somewhat similar to both categories.

Note: Familiarity with this class of drugs is rather limited. Law enforcement and even medical professionals often have to refer to www.erowid.org for information about usage and effects. Much of the material on that pro-drug website is obtained from Dr. Alex Shulgin, known as Papa Ecstasy, who created many of these drugs and has taken and documented all of them as well.

MDMA (ECSTASY)

MDMA — 3,4 METHYLENEDIOXYMETHAMPHETAMINE
Ecstasy, X, XTC, E, The Hug Drug
MDA – 3,4 METHYLENEDIOXY-AMPHETAMINE
(Phenethylamine)

Visual Description:

White or off-white powder or pills. Pills may appear professionally pressed or coarse, homemade. May be a variety of shapes and colors. Seen plain (no logo) or any of 600 cartoons characters, business logos (Mitsubishi, Nike, etc), or symbols (heart, happy face, etc.) Price of a pill varies from $15 to $40; wholesale $6 to $9.

Methods of Use:

Ingested primarily as pills. May be snorted, injected or inserted rectally

Duration of Effects:

Onset: 25-40 minutes
Duration: 4-6 hours desired effects
Impaired for driving up to 12 hours: may have intense fatigue afterwards

Possible Effects:

Nystagmus – Yes
Pupils – Dilated (large)
Pulse – Elevated
Blood Pressure – Elevated
Body Temperature – Elevated
Non-Convergence – No
Altered perception (visual alterations; true hallucinations not likely); altered sense of time
Anxiety
Blurred vision
Bruxism
Chills or sweating
Decreased aggression (unless used poly drug or in high doses)
Depression (after effects wear off or with long-term use)
Dry mouth
Enhanced sense of smell, touch, taste, sight
Enhanced energy; hyperactive
Euphoria
Faintness
Greater self esteem (temporary)
Increased communication (talkative and open)
Lack of inhibitions
Nausea
Paranoia
Sensation of loving all and being loved by all
Sweating

Overdose Symptoms:

Body temperature out of control

Bizarre behavior   Psychosis

Coma   Death

Note: "Ecstasy" has become virtually an umbrella term for a variety of substances in that pills sold as such may contain little or no MDMA (Ecstasy). Related substances (see pages on tryptamines and phenethylamines) may be substituted or included in the pill content. Or the pill may contain meth (for stimulant effect) and LSD or PCP or mescaline (to provide hallucinogenic effect) to simulate MDMA. Or the pill may contain over-the-counter substances such as dextromethorphan (DXM, cough suppressant), ephedrine, or simply pure bunk. The content of MDMA in actual MDMA pills may vary from 50 to 175 mgs (typical pill size is around 300 mgs). Key ingredient for MDMA is safrole (iso-safrole, bromo-safrole or chloro-safrole).

MDA provides more visual disturbance than MDMA and isn't quite as popular. Many of the pills sold as Ecstasy contain only MDA or MDA mixed with other drugs. It should be noted that MDA is also a breakdown product of MDMA in the body. Toxicology results may show a ratio of MDMA to MDA as roughly 85 to 15. That does not in itself indicate ingestion of MDA, but rather ingestion of MDMA metabolizing.

There are more than 600 recognized logos on Ecstasy pills, cartoon characters, business logos, letters, etc. Thus there are many nicknames, typically based on the logo and color or shape of the pill. They do not symbolize a particular dealer or maker. One pill press can produce a variety of logos daily as the metal die with the logo imprint can be readily changed through a pill run.

Death from heatstroke type of event can occur. Users dehydrate and are trained to drink large amounts of water, but excessive water intake during this period can also result in death from hyponatremia, water poisoning.

TRYPTAMINES

DMT

TRYPTAMINES

AMT – Alpha-methyl-tryptamine or Spirals, Amtrak or Amthrax
5-MeO-DIPT —— 5-methoxy-N,N-diisopropyltryptamine or
Foxy or Foxy Methoxy
DMT – Dimethyltryptamine (see DMT page)

There are at least 55 drugs in this category. Most tryptamines occur in nature but all are also synthetically produced. Tryptamines include: **2-Me-DET, 2-Me-DMT, 4-MeO-DIPT, 4-HO-MIPT, 4-HO-DBT, 5-MeO-DMT, DIPT, MBT, 4,5-MDO-DIPT, MBT, AET, DET (analog of DMT)**

Tryptamines commonly recognized as drugs of abuse (but perhaps not commonly known as tryptamines) include Psilocybin (O-phosphoryl-4-hydroxy-N,N-dimethyltryptamine) and psilocyn (4-hydroxy-N, N-dimethyltryptamine) and even LSD.

Visual Description:
Powder or pills, various colors and shapes; with or without logo imprints. AMT is often seen in pills with the oval alien face or spider imprint. Foxy has been found in off-white or orange crystal powder or in capsule or tablet form.

Methods of Use:
Ingested primarily as pills. May be snorted, injected, inserted rectally or smoked.

Duration of Effects:
Varies greatly with the substance taken. AMT lasts 12-24 hours. Foxy 3-6 hours.

Possible Effects:
Pupils – Dilated
Pulse – Elevated
Blood Pressure – Elevated
Body Temperature – Elevated
Visual and auditory distortions
Emotional disturbances

These drugs are hallucinogenic stimulants but with varying effects. Some are more hallucinogenic and some are more stimulant oriented. The effects will be somewhat similar to both categories.

Note: Familiarity with this class of drugs is rather limited. Law enforcement and even medical professionals often have to refer to www.erowid.org for information about usage and effects. Much of the material on that pro-drug website is obtained from Dr. Alex Shulgin, known as Papa Ecstasy, who created many of these drugs and has taken and documented all of them as well.

DMT (DIMETHYLTRYPTAMINE), also known as the "Businessman's Lunch" is one of the most commonly abused tryptamines. It is commonly found in crystalline form, powder or oil, and varies from white to pink to red, w/smell when heated similar to burning plastic

DMT May be snorted, smoked as vapor or mixed with tobacco, marijuana, etc. and smoked, injected, and the effects last approximately 45-60 minutes

Possible Effects:
  Pupils – Dilated
  Pulse – Elevated
  Blood Pressure – Elevated
  Body Temperature – Elevated

Blank stare	Mood changes
Body tremors	Muscle tension
Dazed	Nausea
Disoriented	Perspiring
Flashbacks	Sleeplessness
Hallucinations	Synesthesia
Memory loss	

Overdose Symptoms:
  Bizarre behavior
  Long, intense trips
  Psychosis
  Death

NOTE: 5-MeO-DMT (5-methoxy-N,N-dimethyltryptamine) is related to DMT and comes from certain plants or is synthesized. Smoked or snorted. It is one of the two ingredients excreted by the **Bufo Alvarius toad** (indigenous to southwestern areas of US). This toad excretes venom from glands on its back, containing hallucinogenic substances **bufotenine** and **5-MeO-DMT**. Collected by squeezing the glands; smoke the dried extract. Popularized by the media as licking the toad's back (scaring it first to cause excretion).

JIMSON WEED
(Datura)

Jimson Weed Plant

Jimson Weed Growing Wild

Jimson Weed Pod and Seeds

JIMSON WEED

(Datura)

Visual Description:
Green bush with white trumpet shaped flowers (can range white to purple). The flower pods contain seeds that are consumed. When dried, the pods are light green in color and prickly.

Methods of Use:
Eaten or ingested as tea or smoked

Duration of Effects:
Variable

Possible Effects:
Nystagmus – No
Pupils – Dilated
Pulse – Elevated
Blood Pressure – Elevated
Body Temperature – Elevated
Non-Convergence – No

Blank stare
Body tremors
Delirium
Disoriented
Hallucinations
Impaired divided attention
Mood changes
Memory loss
Muscle tension
Nausea
Perspiring
Sleeplessness
Synesthesia

Overdose Symptoms:
Bizarre behavior
Psychosis
Violence
Death

Note:
Also called angel's trumpet, devil's trumpet, moon flower, Jamestown weed. Active ingredients are the alkaloids hyoscyamine, scopolamine and atropine. Can be very toxic and resulting behavior can be very dangerous.

LSD

(LYSERGIC ACID DIETHYLAMIDE)

Various Forms of LSD

LSD

(LYSERGIC ACID DIETHYLAMIDE)

Visual Description: Varies

Varies – Pure crystals typically clear or white; traditional blotter paper (small squares, perforated sheets, or strips of impregnated paper, often with cartoon characters or artistic designs); on a sugar cube; often seen as a liquid (in small vials such as breath mint, eye or nasal spray, food coloring containers); in gel form as dots on plastic pieces that are sucked; gel form as "pyramids" on, or peeled from, fluorescent light diffuser plastic (used as a mold and then peeled off and cut into strips or perforated first, broken into pieces and sucked). May also be mixed in tablets sold as "Ecstasy" (may contain meth and LSD, if actual MDMA isn't available to achieve similar effects of hallucinogenic stimulant).

Methods of Use:

Ingested; absorbed (skin contact or eye drops). Tiny quantities when in crystalline form (50 micrograms = one hit). Cannot be smoked (destroyed by heat). One ounce of pure LSD equals 567,000 hits, calculated at 50 micrograms each.

Duration of Effects:

Onset – 20-60 minutes
Duration – 6-12 hours

Possible Symptoms:

Nystagmus – No
Pupils – Dilated
Pulse – Elevated
Blood Pressure – Elevated
Body Temperature – Elevated
Non-Convergence – No

Ataxia
Anxiety (bad trip)
Blank stare
Dazed, Disoriented, Delirium
Fear & paranoia (bad trip)
Flashbacks
Hyperthermia (overheating)
Impaired divided attention
Sleeplessness

Impaired sense of time & distance
Increased salivation
Muscle tension
Nausea
Perspiring
Piloerection (goosebumps)
Psychosis
Synesthesia

NOTE: Synesthesia is a condition where one type of stimulation evokes the sensation of another, as when the hearing of a sound produces the visualization of a color)

LSA: D-LYSERGIC ACID AMIDE

(Morning Glory Seeds, Hawaiian Woodrose Seeds)

LSA - D-LYSERGIC ACID AMIDE

(Morning Glory seeds, Hawaiian Woodrose seeds)

Visual Description:
Seeds from Morning Glory (produces variety of flower colors), Hawaiian Woodrose, and Stipa robusta plants, plus ergot fungus.

Methods of Use:
Suck on or swallow seeds.
Grind and soak the seeds and drink the liquid.
Brew tea.

Duration of Effects & Possible Effects:
See LSD; LSA provides similar effects though typically milder.

Note:
This chemical is used in synthesizing LSD. Gives a milder version of an LSD trip.

PEYOTE

Peyote Cactus – Mescaline

Peyote in Capsule Form

Peyote Flower

PEYOTE

Peyote Cactus – Mescaline

Visual Description:
Capsules (gelatin capsules of ground plant material or white crystalline powder if synthesized), needle-shaped translucent crystals, hard brown discs of plant material (the "button" from the plant is removed and dried), tablets.

Methods of Use:
Ingested as capsules or tablets or in soup or tea form; chewed; smoked.

Duration of Effects:
Onset – 30-60 minutes
Duration – 10-12 hours

Possible Symptoms:
Nystagmus – No
Pupils – Dilated
Pulse – Elevated
Blood Pressure – Elevated
Body Temperature – Elevated
Non-Convergence – No

Ataxia
Dazed/Disoriented
Hallucinations
Memory Loss
Psychosis
Rancid Breath
Synesthesia
Sweating
Nausea/Vomiting

Note:
Not illegal for certain members of the Native American Church; used for religious purposes. Documentation of tribal membership and authorization may be required for possession and transportation; verify requirements and department policy in your region.

PSILOCYBIN & PSILOCIN

(Magic Mushrooms)

PSILOCYBIN & PSILOCIN

(Magic Mushrooms)

Visual Description:
Fresh or dried mushrooms (only specific plants); white to brown powder or capsules. Usually stored dry to avoid mold and spoiling.

Methods of Use:
Chewed as plant material, swallowed as a capsule or consumed as tea, ground and smoked mixed with marijuana

Duration of Effects:
Onset – within 20 minutes
Duration – 6-12 Hours

Possible Effects:
Nystagmus – No
Pupils – Dilated
Pulse – Elevated
Blood Pressure – Elevated
Body Temperature – Elevated
Non-Convergence – No

Abdominal pain	Impaired concentration & perception
Ataxia	Muscle tension & twitching
Chills	Nausea
Dazed/Disoriented	Numbness of face, tongue or lips
Difficult or tremulous speech	Synesthesia
Dizziness	Sleeplessness
Euphoria	Slowed passage of time
Fever & Flushing	Psychosis
Hallucinations	Urinary incontinence
Hypertension	Vomiting
	Visualization of patterns with eyes closed

Note:
Growing magic mushrooms for profit is a typically a very high-tech operation with growing beds, elaborate conditions, sterilized fertilizer material, etc. Some mushrooms that may be mistaken for "magic mushrooms" are poisonous. Amanita muscaria mushrooms contain the substances ibotenic acid and muscimol (rather than psilocybin and psilocin), causing similar hallucinogenic reactions but may also be fatal. They have a brown, red or orange cap with white "warts."

SALVIA DIVINORUM

(Active Ingredient Salvinorin A)

SALVIA DIVINORUM
(Active Ingredient Salvinorin A)

Visual Description:
Green plant material (seeds are uncommon; produced from plant cuttings most often). A sage type plant from the mint family.

Methods of Use:
Chewing leaves or drinking tea or soup concoction or smoking. May mix with honey and eat by spoonfuls.

Duration of Effects:
Onset – One minute
Peak – 5-10 minutes
Duration – One hour (Impairment for driving likely for several hours)

Possible Symptoms:
Abdominal Pain
Diarrhea
Difficulty communicating or unable
Euphoria
Hallucinations
Headache/Hangover
Intoxication
Meditative or trance state
Sweaty
Terrifying experiences possible
Uncontrolled laughter at onset
Vomiting
Visual disturbances

Note:
Salvia Divinorum is not illegal typically as of 2005 but growing concern and research is underway. Reportedly Louisiana is the first state to ban it. Some other countries have banned it as well. More hallucinogenic than marijuana and somewhat similar to ingestion of Datura (Jimson Weed), legislation is needed in every state. Sold under such names as "purple sticky" in some head shops around the country and on Internet.

NUTMEG – MYRISTICIN

3-Methoxy-4,5-methylene-dioxyallybenzene and Related Compounds

NUTMEG – MYRISTICIN

3-Methoxy-4,5-methylene-dioxyallybenzene and Related Compounds

Visual Description:
Dried kernel of the myristica fragrans tree, ground for use as a spice.

Methods of Use:
Ingested; usually mixed with liquid to avoid chewing. Some recommend trying to swallow it dry while others recommend orange juice and honey and other recommend frozen concoctions with ice and lemonade. Requires fairly large amounts, such as multiple tablespoons. One pro-drug website nutmeg user recommends 15 grams for a 150 pound person as a starting point, for example.

Duration of Effects:
Onset: From 2 to 8 hours after ingestion
Duration: 24 hours, with minor effects up to 48-72 hours

Possible Effects:
Nystagmus – No
Pupils – Dilated
Pulse – Elevated
Blood Pressure – Elevated
Body Temperature – Elevated
Non-Convergence – No

Ataxia
Constipation
Delirium
Diarrhea
Dry mouth
Euphoria
Flushing
Hallucinations
Hypothermia
Nausea
Psychosis
Synesthesia
Sleepiness afterwards
Tachycardia
Vomiting

Note:
Though not illegal, nutmeg is often banned from correctional institution kitchens. Not widely abused due to more negative than positive effects, but accessible to youth who seek drug experience. Impairs the ability to drive a motor vehicle.

MISCELLANEOUS HALLUCINOGENIC STIMULANTS

Many of these more unusual drugs (TFMPP, BZP, Euphoria and some of the phenethylamines and tryptamines) are seen as powder or crystal form or may be found pressed into pills just like MDMA (Ecstasy) in appearance. The powders may be in nondescript baggies or in vials or bags labeled as "research chemicals."

MISCELLANEOUS HALLUCINOGENIC STIMULANTS

4-methylaminorex — Euphoria or U4EUH; aka: "Ice"

Chemical name:
4,5-dihydro-4-methyl-5-phenyl-2-oxazolamine

Duration of Effects:
Onset: 1-2 hours
Duration: 14-16 hours

Effects:
Intense stimulant with sensations of boundless energy and mental acuity. Enhanced sense of self-esteem. Described by some as a long-lasting MDMA intoxication superimposed with methamphetamine. Other effects: increased respiration, tachycardia, tremors, perspiration, increased blood pressure, intraocular pressure, blurred vision, tightness in the chest, increased body and breath odor. Has not become particularly popular, likely due to the excessiveness of its effects.

PIPERAZINES — BZP & TFMPP

BZP
(Benzylpiperazine)

Sold as a substitute for Ecstasy, MDMA, BZP is a stimulant with some expanded properties, somewhat similar to MDMA, but also with more undesirable side effects. Known as "Poor Man's Ecstasy." Effects last 6-8 hours. BZP is federally scheduled.

TFMPP
(Trifluoromethylphenylpiperazine)

Seen sometimes on its own or mixed with BZP and sold as a recreational drug that is a "legal alternative" to MDMA and/or LSD. Little is known about TFMPP effects. Like BZP it is a stimulant with additional properties. TFMPP is NOT federally scheduled.

This page intentionally left blank.

INHALANTS

INHALANT ABUSE

Two Common Inhalants

INHALANT ABUSE (GENERAL)

Four categories of inhalants:

Solvents – Toluene products, paint/paint thinner, lighter fluid, carburetor cleaner, dry cleaning fluid, correction fluid (some brands), household glue/cement, felt-tip markers, gasoline (benzene), kerosene, fingernail polish remover, grease/spot remover (methylene chloride and toluene)

Aerosols – Spray paint, deodorant, body sprays, room odorizer, hair spray, fabric protector, vegetable cooking spray

Gases – Butane, nitrous oxide and other medical anesthetics (ether, chloroform, halothane), propane, helium, freon

Nitrites – amyl (some medical use re angina), butyl nitrite (video head cleaner), cyclohexyl nitritem (Note: Nitrites are slightly different as they primarily dilate blood vessels and relax the muscles and thus are primarily used as sexual enhancers)

Visual Description:

There are more than 1400 volatile, potentially abusable products on the market today, including hydrocarbons, nitrites, anesthetics, alcohols, and halogen compounds. They are called volatile organic compounds **(VOC)**. They are products never meant for human consumption, such as butane, fabric protector, gasoline, spray paint, hair spray, marking pens, air fresheners, computer keyboard sprays, cleaning agents, starter fluid, fire extinguisher (halon) and glue. Some are inhaled for the named product itself (such as gasoline, glue) while others are abused for the propellant that releases the product (such as nitrous oxide that fires homemade whipped cream makers and propels whipped cream from store-bought cans and cardiac synthesizers that propel air freshener from their containers).

Methods of Use:

Inhaled from a cloth or bag or balloon, or directly from the container

Duration of Effects:

Onset – Rapid   Duration – Brief

INHALANTS

Possible Symptoms (varies with substance) and Signs:

Nystagmus – Varies
Pupils – Normal or Dilated
Pulse – May be Elevated
Blood Pressure – May be Elevated
Body Temperature – Varies with Substance
Non-Convergence – Possibly
Acute Confusion
Agitation
Ataxia
Brain Damage (especially with long-term use)
Brief Euphoria
Cardiac Arrythmia/Failure (especially with fluorocarbons)
Decrease in Appetite
Headaches
Liver & Kidney Damage Possible
Odor of Substance
Poor Memory
Shortness of Breath/Chest Pains
Slurred Speech
Stains on Clothing or Skin
Sores/Rash Around Mouth/Nose
Suicide risk (with persistent use)
Sullen/Lethargic Moods
Tremors
Vomiting

Overdose Symptoms:

Coma   Death

Note: Long-term use can cause weight loss, fatigue, muscle fatigue. Consistent inhaling of vapors can, over time, permanently damage the nervous system. Inhaling while driving is particularly dangerous and has resulted in traffic accidents and deaths. Another indicator is hidden, excessive numbers of spray product containers, chemical-soaked rags or clothing. Testing is difficult due to the brief time period for most of these products.

This page intentionally left blank.

AMYL/BUTYL NITRITE
CYCLOHEXYL NITRITE

AMYL/BUTYL NITRITE/CYCLOHEXYL NITRITE

Visual Description:
Packaged in small bottles, sold as room deodorizers, video head cleaner, etc. Often called "Locker Room," "Rush," "Come," "Brush," etc.

Methods of Use:
Vapors Inhaled

Duration of Effects:
Onset – Rapid
Duration – 2-5 minutes

Possible Symptoms:
Pupils – May be normal or dilated
Pulse – Elevated
Blood Pressure – May be lowered (due to effect of dilating blood vessels)
Body Temperature – May be elevated
Non-Convergence – Possible

Confusion
Disoriented
Flushed head and neck
Headaches
Odor of substance
Slurred speech
Sudden "head rush"

Overdose Symptoms:
Asphyxiation (build-up of inhaled fumes, displacing oxygen in lungs)
Coma
Death

Note:
Long-term use can cause weight loss, fatigue, muscle fatigue. Consistent inhaling of vapors can, over time, permanently damage the nervous system. Amyl nitrite has legitimate medical use re angina. Nitrites are slightly different than other inhalants as they primarily dilate blood vessels and relax the muscles (including the sphincter muscles) and thus are primarily used as sexual enhancers.

NITROUS OXIDE
(Laughing Gas)

NOZ Balloon with
"Cracker" & cartridges

Another form of legitimate
NOZ tanks

NOZ tanks from Rave

NITROUS OXIDE
(Laughing Gas)

Visual Description:
Large dark blue tank (medical grade), medium size bright blue tank (vehicle/motorcycle racing performance enhancement), small metal cylinder (called "whip-its" or "whippets" –often mistaken for CO_2 but slightly shorter and dull silver in color), whipped cream dispenser (spray down for whipped cream; point upward to release the nitrous oxide propellant). May be found with a facemask (to hook via hose to large tanks), balloons (heavier grade than common balloons), or a metal or plastic "cracker" (device to release the gas into balloons from the whip-its). Nitrous Oxide is particularly popular at all-night raves.

Methods of Use:
Inhaled from balloon or tank

Duration of Effects:
Onset – Rapid
Duration – Brief

Possible Effects:
Nystagmus – Possibly
Pupils – Normal or Dilated
Pulse – Elevated
Blood Pressure – Possibly Lowered
Non-Convergence – Possibly
Body Temperature – Depends on Substance

Anemia (chronic use)	Dizziness
Ataxia	Euphoria (brief)
Cardiac arrhythmia	Headache
Confusion	Seizures
Disoriented	Slurred Speech
Injury Due to Falling (brief unconsciousness common)	

Overdose Symptoms:
Coma
Death

Note:
Used in dental practices, nitrous oxide is delivered with a controlled amount of oxygen. Abused from balloons, face masks, etc., the experience is quite different. Oxygen deprivation is the main issue in acute toxicity from nitrous oxide abuse.

INHALANTS

AUTOEROTIC ASPHYXIATION, THE CHOKING GAME & CUTTING

NOTE:

These are practices gaining attention and perhaps increasing in the United States. The desired result is similar to the practice of inhaling—cutting off oxygen to the brain, for as little as sixty seconds, to produce a brief, euphoric altered state of consciousness that some people find pleasurable.

"Autoerotic Asphyxiation" is the act of masturbating and simultaneously choking oneself or being choked into a state of unconsciousness, enhancing sensation. "Erotic Asphyxiation" refers to couples choking each other during sexual acts for enhancement. This is a dangerous practice as the asphyxiation may go too far, resulting in injury or death.

"The Choking Game" has become increasingly popular among youth and is somewhat similar to inhalant abuse as it provides a brief euphoric experience. It's the younger version of sexual practice noted above. They call it things like, "fainting each other" or "dreaming." It produces a brief high and can cause brain damage or death. Indicators are unusual marks around the neck; ties, ropes or belts in unusual configurations; complaints of headaches; blood shot eyes.

"Cutting" or self-mutilation or other forms of self-harm is the act of seeking an altered mood state by inflicting harm serious enough to cause tissue damage to one's own body. It is a non-verbal means of dealing with overwhelming feelings or situations.

NARCOTICS

CODEINE

Tylenol W/Codeine #3
(Brand Name)

Tylenol W/Codeine #4
(Brand Name)

Tylenol W/Codeine #3
(Generic)

Tylenol W/Codeine #4
(Generic)

CODEINE

Trade Names & Combinations

Tylenol w/Codeine
Empirin w/Codeine
Robitussin A-C,
Prometh w/Codeine
Fiorinal (butalbital) w/Codeine

APAP w/Codeine
Codeine w/Promethazine
Phenergan w/Codeine

Visual Description:
Capsules, Dark Liquid (varying in thickness), Tablets

Methods of Use:
Ingested, Injected, Snorted

Duration of Effects:
Onset: 30-60 minutes (oral)
Peak: 1-1.5 hours (oral)
Loaded: 4-6 hours

Possible Symptoms:
Nystagmus – No
Pupils – Constricted
Pulse – Below Normal
Blood Pressure – Below Normal
Body Temperature – Normal/Below Normal
Non-Convergence – No

Depressed Reflexes
Droopy Eyelids (Ptosis)
Drowsiness
Dry Mouth
Euphoria
Fresh Puncture Marks

Impaired Divided Attention
Low, Raspy Voice
Nausea
Poor Muscle Coordination
Profuse Scratching
Vomiting

Overdose Symptoms:

Blurred Vision
Cold, Clammy Skin
Convulsions
Constipation

Rapid, Weak pulse
Slow, Shallow Breathing
Coma
Death

NOTE: Tolerance to narcotics develops quickly, making drug dependence very likely. Phenergan w/codeine is a popular substance of abuse, popularized as "sipping syrup" in rap and hip-hop songs. The cough syrup may be consumed from a baby bottle.

FENTANYL

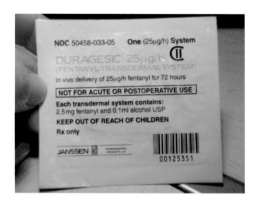

Fentanyl Patch

FENTANYL

Trade Names & Combinations

Alfenta	Sublimaze
Duragesic (patch)	Sufenta
Innovar	

Legitimate fentanyl derivatives

Alfentanyl	Lofentanyl
Fentanyl	Sufentanyl

Illicit analogs

Alpha-methyl fentanyl	benzyl fentanyl
3-methyl fentanyl	

Visual Appearance:
White to tan powder, liquid, patch (prescription)

Methods of Use:
Ingested, injected, snorted

Duration of Effects:
Onset: Rapid w/injection (slower with patch format)
Loaded: 30 minutes to 2 hours (longer in patch format)

Possible Effects:
Nystagmus – No
Pupils – Constricted
Pulse – Below normal
Blood Pressure – Below normal
Body Temperature – Normal or below normal
Non-Convergence – No

Depressed reflexes	Fresh puncture marks
Droopy eyelids (Ptosis)	Impaired divided attention
Drowsiness	Nausea
Dry mouth	Poor muscle coordination
Euphoria	Profuse scratching
Vomiting	

Overdose Symptoms:

Cold, clammy skin	Death
Convulsions	Rapid, weak pulse
Coma	Slow, shallow breathing

Note: Prescription patches contain a concentrated gel that is being extracted and abused. Using the full amount from the patch is likely to be fatal, due to the high dose (intended for transdermal, ongoing transfer, not use all at once). ***Wear gloves when handling open fentanyl patches.*** In 1979 illicit derivatives of fentanyl began appearing in the streets as "China White," a name usually associated with the very pure Southeast Asian heroin.

HEROIN

(Diacetylmorphine)

Asian-China White

Black Tar Heroin
(Black tar-like substance with a vinegar odor)

Columbian Heroin
(powder)

Mexican Brown Heroin
(powder)

Heroin Balloon

Frequently a toy balloon is used to package powdered Heroin. The balloon is used to enable the possessor to swallow the balloon if approached by authorities. It is later retrieved after defecation.

HEROIN
(Diacetylmorphine)

Visual Description:
White to beige or brown powdered substance; or black tar-like substance (chunks may resemble coal, with brown powder clinging to it). May have vinegar odor.

Methods of Use:
Ingested, injected, snorted, smoked (black tar heroin)

Duration of Effects:
Onset: Rapid; varies with route of administration
Intense euphoria 45 seconds to several minutes
Peak: 1-2 hours
Loaded: 3-4 hours (Addicts may inject 2-4 times daily)

Possible Effects:
Nystagmus – No
Pupils – Constricted
Pulse – Below Normal
Blood Pressure – Below Normal
Body Temperature – Normal/Below Normal
Non-Convergence – No

Depressed Reflexes
Droopy Eyelids (Ptosis)
Drowsiness
Dry Mouth
Euphoria
Fresh Puncture Marks

Impaired Divided Attention
Low, Raspy Voice
Nausea
Poor Muscle Coordination
Profuse Scratching
Vomiting

Overdose Symptoms:
Cold, Clammy Skin
Coma
Convulsions
Delirium
Rapid, Weak pulse
Slow, Shallow Breathing

NOTE:
Tolerance to narcotics develops quickly making drug dependence very likely.

HYDROMORPHONE

Dilaudid

HYDROMORPHONE

Dilaudid

Visual Description:
Powder, pills (white, pink, orange, light green, yellow)
1 - 8 mg.

Methods of Use:
Ingested, Injected or Snorted

Duration of Effects:
Onset: 15-30 minutes
Peak: 30-60 minutes
Duration: 4-6 Hours

Possible Effects:
Nystagmus – No
Pupils – Constricted
Pulse – Below Normal
Blood Pressure – Below Normal
Body Temperature – Normal/Below Normal
Non-Convergence – No
Depressed Reflexes
Droopy Eyelids (Ptosis)
Drowsiness
Dry Mouth
Euphoria
Fresh Puncture Marks
Impaired Divided Attention
Low, Raspy Voice
Nausea
Poor Muscle Coordination
Profuse Scratching
Vomiting

Overdose Symptoms:

Cold, Clammy Skin	Slow, Shallow Breathing
Convulsions	Rapid, Weak pulse
Coma	Death

NOTE:
Tolerance to narcotics develops quickly, making drug
dependence very likely.

HYDROCODONE

Hydrocodone & Acetaminophen
(Acetaminophen is the main
ingredient in Tylenol®)

Vicodin (front)

Vicodin (back)

HYDROCODONE

Trade Names & Combinations

Hydrocodone & Acetaminophen - Vicodin, Lorcet, Lortab, Norco

Tussionex cough syrup

Hydrocodone & Aspirin—Damason

Hydrocodone & Homatropine—Hycodan

Hydrocodone & Ibuprofen—Vicoprofen

Visual Description:

Liquid, pills (oblong pills in white, light pink, bright pink, orange, yellow, light blue or red capsules), powder

Methods of Use:

Ingested, injected, snorted

Duration of Effects:

Loaded: 4-8 hours

Possible Effects:

Nystagmus – No

Pupils – Constricted

Pulse – Below normal

Blood Pressure – Below normal

Body Temperature – Normal or below normal

Non-Convergence – No

Depressed reflexes

Droopy Eyelids (Ptosis)

Drowsiness

Dry mouth

Euphoria

Fresh puncture marks

Impaired divided attention

Low, raspy voice

Nausea

Poor muscle coordination

Profuse scratching

Vomiting

Overdose Symptoms:

Cold, clammy skin	Rapid, weak pulse
Convulsions	Slow, shallow breathing
Coma	Death

Note: Tolerance to narcotics develops very quickly, making drug dependence very likely.

MEPERIDINE

MEPERIDINE

Trade Names & Combinations
Demerol
Meperitab

Visual Description:
Tablets (white, 50-100 mg), Clear Liquid, White Powder

Methods of Use:
Ingested, Injected, Snorted

Duration of Effects:
Onset: 10-15 minutes
Peak: 1 hour
Duration: 2-6 Hours

Possible Symptoms:
Nystagmus – No
Pupils – Constricted
Pulse – Below Normal
Blood Pressure – Below Normal
Body Temperature – Normal/Below Normal
Non-Convergence – No

Depressed Reflexes
Droopy Eyelids (Ptosis)
Drowsiness
Dry Mouth
Euphoria
Fresh Puncture Marks
Impaired Divided Attention
Low, Raspy Voice
Nausea
Poor Muscle Coordination
Profuse Scratching
Vomiting

Overdose Symptoms:
Cold, Clammy Skin
Convulsions
Rapid, Weak pulse
Slow, Shallow Breathing
Coma
Death

NOTE:
Tolerance to narcotics develops quickly, making drug
dependence very likely.

METHADONE

(aka Dolophine, Methadose)

Methadone Liquid

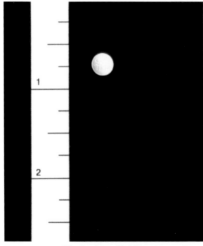

Methadone Tablet

METHADONE

Trade Names
Dolophine
Methadose
Metadol (Canadian)

Visual Description:
Clear, Pink Liquid or White or Peach Tablet, 5-40 mg

Methods of Use:
Ingested, Injected, Snorted

Duration of Effects:
Onset: 30-60 minutes
Duration 4-8 Hours (w/repeated doses, increased to 22-24 hrs

Possible Effects:
Nystagmus – No
Pupils – Possibly Constricted
Pulse – Below Normal
Blood Pressure – Below Normal
Body Temperature – Normal/Below Normal
Non-Convergence – No

Depressed Reflexes
Droopy Eyelids (Ptosis)
Drowsiness
Dry Mouth
Euphoria
Fresh Puncture Marks

Impaired Divided Attention
Low, Raspy Voice
Nausea
Poor Motor Coordination
Vomiting

Overdose Symptoms:
Cold, Clammy Skin
Convulsions
Coma

Rapid, Weak Pulse
Slow, Shallow Breathing
Death

NOTE: When taken in proper doses, Methadone should not show any effects. It is used to keep the Heroin addict "well" and reduce the craving for Heroin. They remain addicted to the opioid, but methadone blocks the high from heroin and does not provide a euphoric rush. It is only effective in cases of addiction to heroin, morphine, and other opioid drugs; it is not an effective treatment for other drugs of abuse. Law enforcement officers are typically familiar only with the use of methadone in heroin addiction treatment. In fact, it is also a pain medication being increasingly widely used by doctors to treat pain and thus even more widely abused. Methadone stays in the system a long time, meaning it can build up and can reach toxic levels. Deaths from methadone overdose have been increasing.

MORPHINE

Morphine Tablets

Morphine Injectable

MORPHINE

Trade Names
MS Contin
Avinza
Roxanol
Duramorph

Visual Description:
Tablets, Pink Liquid

Methods of Use:
Ingested, Injected, Snorted

Duration of Effects:
Onset: Rapid w/injection; 15-60 minutes oral
Peak: 50-90 minutes; 15-60 minutes injected
Impaired: 3-6 Hours

Possible Effects:
Nystagmus – No
Pupils – Constricted
Pulse – Below Normal
Blood Pressure – Below Normal
Body Temperature – Normal/Below Normal
Non-Convergence – No

Depressed Reflexes	Impaired Divided Attention
Droopy Eyelids (Ptosis)	Low, Raspy Voice
Drowsiness	Nausea
Dry Mouth	Poor Motor Coordination
Euphoria	Profuse Scratching
Fresh Puncture Marks	Vomiting

Overdose Symptoms:
Cold, Clammy Skin
Convulsions
Rapid, Weak Pulse
Slow, Shallow Breathing
Coma
Death

NOTE:
Tolerance to narcotics develops quickly making drug
dependence very likely.

OPIUM

Opium Poppy Showing cuts to extract the raw
Opium

OPIUM

Visual Description:
Dark Brown Chunks, Powder

Methods of Use:
Injected, Ingested (liquid, tea), Smoked, Snorted

Duration of Effects:
Impaired: 4-6 Hours

Possible Effects:
Nystagmus – No
Pupils – Constricted
Pulse – Below Normal
Blood Pressure – Below Normal
Body Temperature – Normal/Below Normal
Non-Convergence – No

Depressed Reflexes	Impaired Divided Attention
Droopy Eyelids (Ptosis)	Low, Raspy Voice
Drowsiness	Nausea
Dry Mouth	Poor Motor Coordination
Euphoria	Profuse Scratching
Fresh Puncture Marks	Vomiting

Overdose Symptoms:
Apnea
Cold, Clammy Skin
Convulsions
Delirium
Pulmonary Edema
Rapid, Weak Pulse
Slow, Shallow Breathing
Coma
Death

NOTE:
Tolerance to narcotics develops quickly making drug
dependence very likely.

OXYCODONE

Percocet

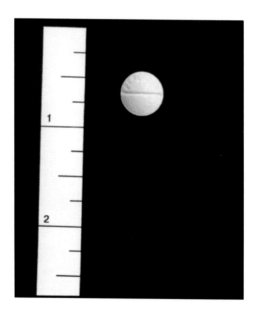

Percodan

OXYCODONE

Common Trade Names & Combinations

Oxycodone: OxyContin, Oxydose, OxyFast, Tylox

Oxycodone & Acetaminophen: Percocet, Roxicet, Endocet, Oxycocet (Canadian)

Oxycodone & Aspirin: Percodan, Endodan, Oxycodan (Canadian)

Visual Description:

Tablets, Drops, Liquid

Methods of Use:

Ingested, Injected, Snorted

Duration of Effects:

Onset: 15-30 minutes (oral)

Impaired: 4-6 Hours

Possible Effects:

Nystagmus – No

Pupils – Constricted

Pulse – Below Normal

Blood Pressure – Below Normal

Body Temperature – Normal/Below Normal

Non-Convergence – No

Depressed Reflexes	Impaired Divided Attention
Droopy Eyelids (Ptosis)	Low, Raspy Voice
Drowsiness	Nausea
Dry Mouth	Poor Motor Coordination
Euphoria	Profuse Scratching
Fresh Puncture Marks	Vomiting

Overdose Symptoms:

Cold, Clammy Skin

Convulsions

Rapid, Weak Pulse

Slow, Shallow Breathing

Coma

Death

NOTE:

Tolerance to narcotics develops quickly making drug dependence very likely.

ADDITIONAL NARCOTICS

Butorphanol Tartrate - Stadol

Propoxyphene & Acetaminophen - Darvocet

ADDITIONAL NARCOTICS

Drug name – Trade name (representative)

Buprenorphine—Buprenex, Subutex 7-24 hours duration
Butorphanol Tartrate—Stadol (nasal spray) 3-6 hours duration
Propoxyphene & acetaminophen—Darvocet 4-6 hours duration
Propoxyphene—Darvon, Darvon-N 4-6 hours duration
Nalbuphine—Nubain 3-6 hours duration
Pentazocine—Talwin, Talacen, Talwin NX 2-3 hours duration
Tramadol—Ultram 6-8 hours duration

NOTE: Effects generally similar to other narcotic analgesics

This page intentionally left blank.

DISSOCIATIVE ANESTHETICS

PCP

(Phencyclidine)

Powdered PCP

PCP in Liquid Form

PCP

Dissociative Anesthetics
(Phencyclidine)

Visual Description:

White or brown powder, pills, capsules, light to medium gold liquid. Occasionally found mixed with meth in pills sold as Ecstasy

Methods of Use:

Ingested; smoked (marijuana or tobacco cigarette dipped in PCP); absorbed; inhaled; injected.

Duration of Effects:

Onset: 1-5 Minutes   Loaded: 4-6 Hours
Peak: 15-30 Minutes
Overdose Effects: 24 Hrs or Longer

Possible Effects:

Nystagmus – Yes (Vertical & Horizontal)
Pupils – Near Normal
Pulse – Elevated
Blood Pressure – Elevated
Body Temperature – Elevated
Non-Convergence – Yes

Agitation & Aggressive
Analgesia (pain block, high pain threshold)
Catatonia
Cyclic Behavior
Disoriented
Dysphoria
Eyelid Tremors
Emergence Delirium
Fearful
Fascination w/Water

Long, Intense Trips

Muscle Rigidity
Non-Communicative
Odor of Substance
Paranoia
Perspiring
Repetitive Speech
Synesthesia
Warm to the Touch

Overdose Symptoms:

Bizarre Behavior
Long, Intense Trips
Psychosis
Violence
Death

KETAMINE (SPECIAL K)

Common T-Shirt Logo

Legitimate (left) and Counterfeit
(right) Ketamine Vials

Ketamine Vial and Powder

KETAMINE (SPECIAL K)

Visual Description:
Clear liquid (very light amber color) often in injectable type vial; white powder

Methods of Use:
Ingested; snorted; smoked; injected; rectal insertion.

Duration of Effects:
Onset: rapid
Pain Block: 30 minutes to 2 hours (dose dependent)
Amnesia effect up to 2 hours

Possible Effects:
Nystagmus – yes
Pupils – Near normal
Pulse – Elevated
Blood Pressure – Elevated
Body Temperature – Elevated
Non-Convergence – Yes

Analgesia (pain block)
Apnea
Catatonic state (The K-Hole)
Delirium
Emergence delirium (bizarre or violent behavior)
Flashbacks
Hallucinations (vivid)
Insomnia
Seizures
Tremors
Vomiting
Coma
Cardiac arrest

Note: Avoid stimulation such as loud noises and rapid movements around subjects under the influence to reduce emergence delirium. May have flashbacks.

DEXTROMETHORPHAN

Common Commercial DXM Products

Common Liquid DXM Product

DXM – Street Name "Triple C" Tablets

DEXTROMETHORPHAN
(DXM)
Cough Suppressant

DXM is a common ingredient as a cough suppressant in numerous over-the-counter products and is not a controlled substance at this time. It is a highly abused substance nationwide, especially among young teens because of its legal availability. Even teens with money to buy the product sometimes shoplift because this act is virtually part of the culture of the DXM crowd. Normal dosing involves one or two pills or doses of cough syrup every four hours. Abusers may take 10 to 45 pills at a time or fairly rapid succession as they seek to achieve the various "plateaus" of experiences described on Internet websites such as www.dextroverse.org and www.erowid.org, two of many pro-drug websites. Some rank DXM with depressants but in higher doses, it is closer in effects to PCP and ketamine, making it an atypical dissociative anesthetic or narcotic analgesic. The effects are also complicated by the fact that it is often taken in pills with other ingredients as well, causing variations on effect. Websites instruct abusers on extracting DXM from cough syrups and pills that contain other medications to avoid the interactions and high doses of the other ingredients.

Duration:
> Onset 15-30 minutes (oral), more rapid if snorted
> Duration 6 hours

Visual Description:
> Gel capsule, pill or liquid, varying with product, and may be seen in powder form.

Possible Effects:

Excitation	Hypertension
Respiratory depression	Hyperthermia
Insomnia	Ataxia
Coma	Tremors
Fever	Hyperactivity, and in high doses dissociative effects similar to PCP or ketamine

Terms & Products:
> Robotripping, Robitussin DM, Coricidin Cough & Cold (aka CCC, Triple C), The Matrix (for the red CCC pills), Skittles and Skittling, DexAlone, Simply Cough, Vicks 44 Cough Relief, Benylin, Creomulsion Cough, ElixSure, Silphen DMetc. Any product containing DXM is a potential target for abuse. DexAlone contains no other ingredients.

This page intentionally left blank.

STIMULANTS

AMPHETAMINES

Drug Name – Representative Tradename

Amphetamine and Dextroamphetamine – Adderall

Dextroamphetamine – Dexedrine, Dextrostat (Canada)

Methylphenidate – Ritalin, Concerta, Metadate,
Riphenidate (Canada)

Pemoline – Cylert (no longer marketed in the US)

Methamphetamine – Desoxyn

Visual Description:

Various shapes/colors/doses of capsules or pills, depending on brand and dosage. May also be found in powder.

Methods of Use:

These are prescription drugs typically used for treatment of attention deficit disorders, narcolepsy or exogenous obesity. But they have become widely diverted as stay-awake pills for students, working adults, etc. Abusers may take them as pills or crush them into powder for snorting or even convert to liquid for injecting.

Duration of Effects:

Onset: 30 seconds (snorted/injected) to 1½ hours (oral)

Duration: 4-8 hours (Concerta is a slow-release version of Ritalin)

Possible Effects:

Nystagmus – No	**Blood Pressure** – Elevated
Pupils – Dilated	**Body Temperature** – Elevated
Pulse – Elevated	**Non-Convergence** – No
Anxiety	Headaches
Arrhythmia	Hypertension
Body tremors	Impaired divided attention
Decreased appetite	Increased alertness
Dizziness	Insomnia
Dry mouth	Psychomotor agitation or retardation
Euphoria	Restlessness
Excitation	Sexual impairment
Grinding teeth (bruxism)	Sweating
Hallucinations	Weight loss

Overdose Symptoms:

Convulsions	Vomiting
Coma	Seizures
Death	

Note: High levels of amphetamines or injected doses can create a sudden rise in blood pressure that can cause a stroke, very high fever or heart attack. Prolonged use can cause hallucination, delusions and paranoia. Even chewing tablets versus swallowing can increase side effects and decrease efficacy for those using legitimately. Pemoline dropped due to increased liver function risks.

COCAINE

(Crack or Freebase)

Cocaine - Crack or Freebase

Cocaine - 18th Street Style

Cocaine - Dope, Money and the Gun

COCAINE

(Crack or Freebase)

Visual Description:
Light brown, beige or white crystalline rocks often packaged in small vials or zip-lock plastic bags. May also be found in "cookie" shapes when made in the bottom of small containers and not yet broken/cut into pieces. Though most often made with baking soda, coke powder may also be converted with baking soda, flour, yeast and carbonated beverage, resulting in a more bubbled texture.

Methods of Use:
Smoked

Duration of Effects:

Onset:	8-30 seconds	Duration:	10-20 minutes
Peak:	5 minutes		

Possible Effects:
Nystagmus – No
Pupils – Dilated
Pulse – Elevated
Blood Pressure – Elevated
Body Temperature – Elevated
Non Convergence – No

Anxiety	Hallucinations
Apnea	Hypertension
Ataxia	Impaired divided attention
Body tremors	Impotence
Decreased appetite	Increased alertness
Dental erosion (chronic use)	Insomnia
Depression	Paranoia
Dizziness	Restlessness
Dry mouth	Running/Red/Bleeding Nose
Euphoria	Seizures
Excitation	Sweating
Fresh puncture marks	Talkative
Grinding teeth (bruxism)	Weight loss
Headaches	

Overdose Symptoms:

Agitation, extreme	Coma
Convulsions	Death

Notes: The 18th Street Gang is known for its signature "wafer" rock cocaine, shaped in thin squares or rectangles resembling wafers or pasta, rather than the traditional "rock" shapes. Traditional rock cocaine somewhat resembles pieces of macadamia nut, though harder in texture.

Freebasing cocaine using ether is a less common and much more dangerous method (severe burns can result if smoked before the ether has completely evaporated). Waxy or soapy in appearance.

COCAINE

Cocaine Powder

Powdered Cocaine is placed on a mirror or piece of glass or other flat, non-porous surface. It is then chopped into a fine powder with a razor blade or credit card. The Cocaine is then spread into thin lines, and the lines are then snorted through a tube, drinking straw or rolled currency. (See page 133)

Kilos of Cocaine

COCAINE

Powder

Visual Description:
White crystalline (shiny) powder (may be "cut" or diluted with other products such as procaine, lidocaine, mannitol, ephedrine, sucrose, lactose, tetracaine, benzocaine, etc., to extend the quantity of product). Has surfaced as "black" cocaine to attempt to fool law enforcement, using charcoal, cobalt, iron dust, etc., to alter the color. May be found in bindles, plastic baggies, or pressed into kilos. Markings on kilos may indicate the producer or the intended recipient.

Methods of Use:
Snorted. Injected. (Chewing coca leaf provides a mild stimulant effect).

Duration of Effects:

Onset: Injected – immediate	Snorted – 2-3 minutes
Oral – within 1 hour	
Loaded: 5-45 minutes	Oral ingestion: 1-2 hours
Peak: 5-15 minutes	

Possible Effects:

Nystagmus – No   **Pupils** – Dilated
Pulse – Elevated   **Blood Pressure** – Elevated
Body Temperature – Elevated
Non-Convergence – No

Anxiety	Hallucinations
Apnea	Hypertension
Ataxia	Impotence
Body tremors	Impaired divided attention
Decreased appetite	Increased alertness
Dental erosion (chronic use)	Insomnia
Depression	Paranoia
Dizziness	Restlessness
Dry mouth	Running/Red/Bleeding Nose
Euphoria	Seizures
Excitation	Sweating
Fresh puncture marks	Talkative
Grinding teeth (bruxism)	Weight loss
Headaches	

Overdose Symptoms:

Agitation, extreme	Convulsions
Coma	Death

Note: Occasional use of cocaine can cause an irritated, stuffy or blood nose, while long-term use may result in ulceration of the mucous membranes of the nose or complete perforation of the nasal septum. Schedule II because it does have limited legitimate use as a topical anesthesia of the mucous membranes for medical procedures.

METHAMPHETAMINE

(Crank or Speed)

ICE

Varied Colors of Methamphetamine

METHAMPHETAMINE

Visual Description:
Powder or chunks of various shades from white to beige, orange or pink (dye from type of source pills used for ephedrine or pseudoephedrine). Like cocaine, it may be adulterated with "cuts" to extend the quantity or to clean up the color; common cut is a dietary supplement MSM (methyl-sulfonyl methane). Also marketed in prescription tablet as Desoxyn for short-term weight loss and attention deficit disorder.

"Ice" or crystal meth: white crystalline rock; freebase form of methamphetamine, typically of high purity. May look like chunks of ice or shards of glass.

Methods of Use:
Injected, smoked, snorted, swallowed

Duration of Effects:
Onset: 5-20 minutes (snorted) 30-60 minutes (oral) within seconds (smoked)
Duration: 6-18 hours

Possible Effects:
Nystagmus – No
Pupils – Dilated
Pulse – Elevated
Blood Pressure – Elevated
Body Temperature – Elevated
Non-Convergence – No

Anxiety	Increased alertness
Body tremors	Insomnia
Decreased appetite	Loss of coordination
Dizziness	Paranoia
Dry mouth	Puncture marks
Euphoria	Restlessness
Excitation	Sexual stimulation
Grinding teeth (bruxism)	Sweating
Hallucinations	Weight loss
Impaired divided attention	

Overdose Symptoms:

Agitation	Hallucinations
Coma	Psychosis
Convulsions	Death

Note: Methamphetamine can be made in a variety of ways, depending on the quantity being made and the materials available. Large meth labs may involve extensive chemical lists and laboratory equipment; small labs may involve only easily obtained ingredients and homemade conversion of common items. "Ice" is crystal meth, a smokable form of methamphetamine. Use first started in the Far East, then Hawaii, with use/manufacturing based in South Korea, the Philippines, Honk Kong and Japan. Now found in a much more widespread pattern in the US.

METHCATHINONE

(Synonym N-Methyl-Cathinone, aka "Cat")

METHCATHINONE

(Synonym N-Methyl-Cathinone, aka "Cat")

Visual Description:
Off-white, light yellow or beige powder

Methods of Use:
Injected, snorted, smoked or taken orally

Duration of Effects:
Loaded from 30 minutes to 24 hours depending on dosage

Possible Effects:
Nystagmus – No
Pupils – Dilated
Pulse – Elevated
Blood Pressure – Elevated
Body Temperature – Elevated
Non-Convergence – No

Anxiety
Body tremors
Decreased appetite
Dizziness
Euphoria
Excitation
Grinding teeth (bruxism)
Hallucinations
Impaired divided attention
Increased alertness
Insomnia
Loss of coordination
Paranoia
Puncture marks
Restlessness

Overdose Symptoms:
Agitation
Convulsions
Fever
Hallucinations
Psychosis
Coma
Death

Note: Though easily made and similar to methamphetamine, this drug has been mostly centered in the Midwest and not widely favored. Just as with methamphetamine, ephedrine or pseudoephedrine is the key ingredient. Norephedrine (phenylpropanolamine) can be substituted, resulting in cathinone rather than methcathinone (see cathinone).

CATHINONE

(Also Khat – Catha Edulis Plant)

Khat - Rolled and Tied for Distribution

CATHINONE

Also Khat – Catha Edulis plant
(Pronounced "Cot")

Visual Description:
White powder if synthesized (similar to making methamphetamine or methcathinone). Or, plant material from a flowering evergreen tree or large shrub. Leaves are described as green to crimson-brown and glossy, but may become yellow-green and leathery as they age/dry.

Methods of Use:
Chewing the leaves, drinking plant juice

Duration of Effects:
Onset: 20 minutes   Duration: 2 hours

Possible Effects:
Nystagmus – No
Pupils – Dilated
Pulse – Elevated
Blood Pressure – Elevated
Body Temperature – Elevated
Non-Convergence – No

Anesthetic properties
Anxiety
Body tremors
Decreased appetite
Dizziness
Euphoria

Excitation
Impaired divided attention
Increased alertness
Insomnia
Paranoia
Restlessness

Overdose Symptoms:
Breathing difficulties
Convulsions
Psychosis
Coma
Death

Note: Plant comes primarily from Eastern Africa at high altitudes. Khat contains cathinone when leaves are fresh. As leaves dry (unrefrigerated more than 48 hours), contents deteriorate to contain only cathine, a lesser stimulant.

ADDITIONAL STIMULANTS

Diethylpropion - Tenuate

Phentermine
Courtesy of: Christine Larson, AZDPS

ADDITIONAL STIMULANTS
Drug Name – Representative Tradename

Diethylpropion – Tenuate, Dospan
(anorectic - for weight loss, stimulant effects)
Mazindol – Mazanor, Sanorex (anorectic
for weight loss and narcolepsy)
Phenmetrazine – Nistenal, Preludin (anorectic)
Phendimetrazine – Prelu-2 (anorectic)
Benzphetamine – Didrex (anorectic)
Phentermine – Adipex, Fastin, Ionamin (anorectic)
Fenfluramine or Dexfenfluramine – Pondimin, Redux

Visual Description:
Various pills, capsules or powder

Methods of Use:
Taken as pills or snorted

Duration of Effects:
Similar to other stimulants, varying with product

Possible Effects:
Similar to other stimulants

Note: Fen Phen, a once popular diet pill combination, was a combination of phentermine and fenfluramine or dexfenfluramine that was linked to excessive cases of primary pulmonary hypertension, resulting in numerous lawsuits.

Additional Stimulant w/Unique Properties
Modafinil – Provigil (daytime sleepiness, narcolepsy)

Note: Modafinil is said to be relatively free of typical stimulant side effects such as agitation, irritability, nervousness, euphoria or the potential for paranoid delusion and addiction that are common to other stimulants (when used a directed). Modafinil targets very specific regions of the brain believed to regulate normal wakefulness. This drug is being touted for shift-work related sleepiness. While "abuse" may not follow traditional stimulant patterns, over use of it may result in fatigue after the fact and thus result in impaired driving. Effects may include blurred vision, dizziness, dry mouth, insomnia, depression, confusion, mood swings, nervousness, anxiety or agitation, etc.

Taurine Containing Drinks

caplet contains: 12 mg ephedrine group alkaloids
40 mg caffeine alkaloids

ADDITIONAL STIMULANTS
Other Chemicals With Stimulant Properties

Ephedrine & Pseudoephedrine (also Ma Huang)
Bitter Orange - citrus aurantium (synephrine)
Kola nut extract
Taurine (featured in large quantity in numerous energy drinks)
Caffeine (also called Guarana)
Yohimbe

NOTE: These chemicals may cause typical stimulant properties such as increased heart rate, increased body temperature, etc., and may be encountered in DUI or overdose cases. Bitter orange, kola nut, taurine and caffeine are often included in supplements in very large quantities as ephedrine alternatives or in addition to ephedrine, but may harbor some of the same risk factors as taking ephedrine. Relatively little research has been done re ongoing ingestion of large quantities of such ingredients.

This page intentionally left blank.

PARAPHERNALIA
IDENTIFICATION AND
DESCRIPTIONS

ASSORTED SMOKING PARAPHERNALIA

BINDLE

Explanation: A bindle is a small piece of paper or currency, folded like an envelope to form a pocket, used to hold a personal amount of a drug.

CLOTHES THAT HIDE DRUGS

It isn't just in the hat band any more. Hats are made with hidden compartments in the area behind the logo, opening from inside the band with Velcro. Others have entire top sections with Velcro entry on the inside.

420 stands for marijuana—references planting marijuana on 4-20, the universal beginning of growing season.

These items are innocent in themselves but it is important to do a thorough search and anticipate unusual hiding spots.

Shoes have been found with carved-out areas in the sole, under the insert (commercially made as well as homemade) and in the side zip pockets (styles/brands common for kids and large enough for little more than a key or small quantities of dope. One pair was found at a rave with a zipper completely around the tongue, opening to a large compartment.

Shirts and pants also come with numerous hidden features. Caffeine brand clothing features the "e" at the end backwards in their logo, similar to the concept of "flipping E," meaning doing the drug Ecstasy with other drugs—poly drug use. Caffeine and Kikwear clothing brands cater to the rave crowd. Velcro pockets may be found in the side seams or hem of shirts and pants. Some pants feature a hidden Velcro compartment on the inner leg seam, for example.

CLOTHING INDICATES DRUG PREFERENCE

There is an endless stream of clothing and logos indicating drug preference and covers all drugs. Note the Ecstasy, Rated X and EXXTC, all indicating love for the drug MDMA. Special K refers to the animal tranquilizer ketamine.

COCAINE SIFTER

METHODS OF USE:

The drug is placed in the top compartment. The lid is screwed on and the handle is turned, forcing the powder through the screen. The result is a powder with a very fine texture for snorting

Powdered cocaine is placed on a mirror, piece of glass or other flat, non-porous surface. If not already in fine powder, it's typically chopped with a razor blade or credit card. It is then combed into fine lines with the razor or credit card...

...the lines are then commonly snorted through a straw or rolled paper or dollar bill, or by use of a small spoon.

COPPER SCOURING PADS

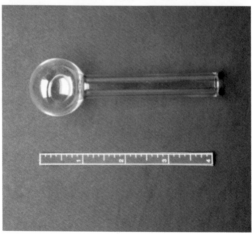

METHODS OF USE:

Small, round pieces of these pads are placed in bowls of Freebase Pipes. The **"rock"** is then placed on top of the pad and lit. The metal fibers of the pad hold the melting **"rock"** and keep it hot. The most popular brand of copper is **"Chore Boy"**. Very fine steel wool or **"Brillo pads"** are also used.

DRUG LAB

Methamphetamine Lab

Typical Items Found at Meth Lab

Methamphetamine can be made by a variety of recipes and methods. Simple methods render small quantities and more elaborate productions result in huge quantities. Bottom line, though, the main ingredients are common in households and stores, ephedrine or psuedoephedrine pills, Coleman cooking fuel, lithium batteries (the lithium is removed from the case and is highly flammable), etc.

FREEBASE SMOKING PIPE

METHODS OF USE:

After placing a piece of copper scouring pad, steel wool or Brillo Pad in the bowl, the Freebase Rock is placed on top and lit. The rock will begin to vaporize and melt. Since the vapors are heavier than air, they drop into the neck of the pipe and are drawn into the lungs. Some pipes have a bulge or chamber in the neck of the pipe that is used to collect the vapor and allow it to accumulate before it is inhaled into the lungs. This chamber is also used for cooling the vapor. A glass or metal tube, called a **"Straight Shooter"** is also used. Often made from automotive radio antennas, they are readily obtained and can be easily dropped if authorities should approach.

See WASHBACK METHODS on Page 155

HEROIN PARAPHERNALIA

EXPLANATION:

Powdered or Tar Heroin is placed in the "cooker", water is added, and solution is heated. A piece of cotton is added to act as a filter and the solution is drawn up into the needle. The arm is then "tied-off" with a belt, cord, or bandana to bulge the vein. The bulging of the vein is for easy injection and to cause the "rush" after the "tie-off" is released.

The "cooker" is most often made from a spoon or bottom of an aluminum drink can.

This injection process is the same for Cocaine and/or Methamphetamine injections except the drugs are not heated because they are water soluble. They are placed in the cooker and warm water is added.

NOTE:

The "cottons" are kept. When the user does not have drugs, he will use the "cottons" to extract what ever small amount of Heroin is left in them. Cottons are considered drug residue and are not against the law to possess in some states.

HEROIN

(CONTAINED IN A TOY BALLOON)

METHOD OF PACKAGING & TRANSPORTING:
Frequently a toy balloon is used to package Mexican powdered Heroin. The balloon allows the possessor to swallow the balloon if approached by authorities. It is later retrieved after is passes through the body's digestive system. (Shown next to a dime only to illustrate size.)

MARIJUANA ROACH CLIPS

METHODS OF USE:
   "Roach Clips" are used to hold the last bit of a burning Marijuana cigarette. In addition to the devices shown, small tweezers may also be used.

METHAMPHETAMINE (ICE) SMOKING PIPES

A commercial auto air freshener is emptied and the end of the tube is heated and blown into, creating a bulge at the end. A hole is poked through the bulging end with a hot needle.

METHAMPHETAMINE (ICE) SMOKING PIPES

The end of a light bulb is cut off and the insides discarded. A hole is poked in the round end with a hot needle

METHODS OF USE:

A small piece of the drug is placed inside the round portion of the pipe. The round portion is then heated from beneath, which causes creates vapors. There is a small hole at the top of the round portion of the pipe. The user places a finger over the hole, allowing the vapors to accumulate. The finger is then removed and the vapor is drawn into the lungs. Meth smokers often have a round burn mark on the finger used to block the bowl.

NITROUS OXIDE PARAPHERNALIA

Nitrous oxide canisters (smaller than CO_2 cylinders) are common in gourmet coffee shops because they propel the whipped cream from homemade whipped cream containers. Nitrous can be abused from the store's whipped cream makers just as it can from commercial cans of whipped cream (holding the can down releases whipped cream, holding it up releases the propellant, nitrous oxide). Employees have been known to slip a canister or two in the bottom of a large cup and then double cup the drink to send nitrous out with a friend

NITROUS OXIDE PARAPHERNALIA

NITROUS OXIDE PARAPHERNALIA

"Crackers" are devices used to puncture the whippets and fill balloons with nitrous oxide to then inhale. Most are aluminum or brass and the manufacturing quality resembles flashlights used by police. But they also come in plastic and can be made from standard PVC fittings (described on the Internet). The balloons are heavy duty, not typical party balloon quality. With the larger tanks of nitrous oxide (from dental offices, dental supply houses or the medium size from high performance vehicle shops), abusers may use the top half of a 2-liter soda bottle as an inhalation mask, attaching it to the tank with a piece of tubing. Inhaling directly from the tanks is dangerous as nitrous oxide gets very cold and can cause damage to lungs, etc. from the intense cold.

RAVE PARAPHERNALIA

MDMA (Ecstasy) enhances all of the senses, making everything pleasurable, including loud noises (users will cling to the speakers for the sound and vibration), touch (may fondle ordinary surfaces and find them fascinating), smell (love the smell of methanol chest rubs to enhance the act of breathing), sights (fascinated by flashing lights, for example), etc.

Ravers give each other "light shows" with various spinning or flashing lights. Using the photon lights, visible up to one mile, in their eyes at close proximity may cause damage.

Vibrators, massages, the odor of vapor rub enhances their pleasure.

MDMA causes bruxism, teethgrinding; users suck on lollipops, pacifiers, glow sticks, etc., to try to reduce the teethgringing and jaw locking.

Rave flyers are coded with images or phrases familiar to them and often overlooked by police, teachers and parents. The flyer doesn't say ONE, it says, "On Ecstasy;" Note the lower case "o" and "n" but the capital "E." Cand E Flip refers to the flip (practice of mixing MDMA with another drug) of using both LSD and MDMA. "E" or "X" will be highlighted, underlined, capitalized, etc., to accentuate it.

Regular containers may be used to hide their drugs. PEZ containers may harbor MDMA pills or may contain actual PEZ candy laced with liquid LSD. MDMA pills may be found pressed into Tootsie Roll candies to get them past the eyes of teachers, cops and parents. These have also been used to smuggle black tar heroin into jail facilities. MDMA pills have been found intermingled with the candies on candy necklaces.

SCALES

Pocket Drug-Weighing Scale

Common Drug Weighing Scale

These scales are often used by dealers who sell in small quantities (such as a gram). The dealers are often called **"Pocket Dealers"**. The scale is assembled and the amount desired is set on the slide arm. The drug is then added to the bowl until the arm is level.

SNORTING SPOON

METHODS OF USE:

The desired amount of the drug is placed in the bowl of spoon (top in this photo). One nostril is closed while the other nostril is used to snort the drug from the spoon.

SNORTING TUBE

METHODS OF USE:

The desired amount of the drug is placed on a smooth surface, such as a piece of glass or a mirror. A razor blade or straight edge, such as a credit card, is used to chop the drug into fine particles. A **"line"** is then made with the substance. The tube is placed into one nostril while the other nostril is closed. The drug is then shorted through the tube into the nose.

Snorting tubes may be made from glass or metal tubing. Often they are made from a tightly rolled twenty dollar bill, which results in the presence of drug residue on the bill.

SNORTING VIALS

SNORTING VIALS

METHODS OF USE:

The snorting vial consists of a small vial with a spoon-like device attached to the top. The drug is carried in the vial and a small amount is placed in the "spoon". One nostril is closed and the drug is snorted into the other nostril. In the device above, a small bowl is drilled into the top and the drug is snorted from that bowl.

STASH CANS

STASH CANS

METHODS OF USE:

These cans are used to hold small quantities of drugs. Name brand product cans are modified to allow removal of the top or bottom end of the can. Threads may be "reversed" which makes the can appear normal when an attempt to unscrew the end by twisting in a counter-clockwise rotation.

Stash cans may include beer or soft drink cans, aerosol containers, shaving cream cans or any number of other common household products.

WASHBACK METHODS

As Cocaine vapors travel the length of the pipe, some of the vapors dry and adhere to the sides of the pipe. The following processes are popular street methods for retrieving usable Cocaine that is trapped inside the pipe.

WET WASH METHOD:

A small amount of "151" Rum is put into the mouthpiece of the pipe and the inside is washed out. The rum is then poured on a mirror or a piece of glass and ignited, burning off some of the rum. A piece of copper pad, Brillo pad or steel wool is rubbed on the glass to soak up what is left after burning. The pad is then placed in the pipe, lit, and the vapors drawn into the lungs.

DRY WASH METHOD:

A small amount of "151" Rum is put into the mouthpiece of the pipe and the inside is washed out. The rum is then poured on a mirror or a piece of glass and ignited. The rum is burned until it is completely dry. What is left on the glass or mirror is usable Cocaine. This residue is scrapped off the glass, placed in the pipe and smoked.

The Dry Wash Method is the most popular. These Washback Methods are primarily used with a Freebase Cocaine Pipe, but may also be used with an ICE or Methamphetamine Pipe.

NEEDLE INJECTIONS/
PUNCTURE WOUNDS

STERILE INJECTIONS

after 30 minutes

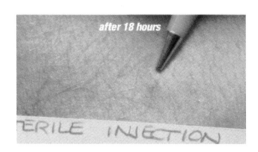

after 18 hours

UNSTERILE INJECTIONS

NEEDLE INJECTIONS

Heroin addicts prefer injecting directly into the vein for the most rapid, intense high. Physicians, on the other hand, most commonly inject narcotics under the skin or in muscle. The addict will inject virtually anywhere, either to attempt to hide the marks from view or because the scarring that builds up from chronic use necessitates venturing far and wide to find injection sites. They typically start with the arm and back of the hand but eventually may use ankles, calves, thighs, the groin area, lower portion of the lip, etc. Done properly and with sterile equipment, the injection side will be minor and heal quickly. But, most heroin addicts have marks, scabs, abscesses and scar tissue over their veins from repeated injections under non-sterile, non-hygienic circumstances.

After the "fix" a small pinkish swelling will occur at the injection point. The swelling may appear as a tiny hole and may have fresh blood around it. Within 24 hours an infection may set in from non-sterile conditions. After a day so, the clotting blood and body serums form an orange-pink scab. The first scab would be slightly smaller than the head of a pin, round in shape with raised pink tissue in the center. There may be a bruised area around it if the user is inexperienced or careless. There may be an elongated area if a dull or bent needle was used. If the needle was dirty, there may be a black or blue tinge from the dirt or soot from the needle having been heated with a match. The surrounding tissue may be reddened and could have significant swelling. Two or three days later, the scab will become more orange and swelling reduced. The scab darkens as it ages. After about ten days the scab may flake off. There may be multiple marks of about the same age if the user injects repeatedly throughout the day or misses and has to try again. If the same site is used repeatedly, the scab will be larger and the area more traumatized. Scarring can become significant, forming visible "tracks" of the users historical injection sites. Abscesses may form from the unsanitary conditions and veins can collapse from the ongoing abuse.

Over the years, fear of needles and the growing risk of contracting HIV and other diseases made heroin abuse less attractive to the younger and richer set. But the availability of smokable, black tar heroin caused an increase in heroin abuse in wider circles.

This page intentionally left blank.

APPENDIX

DRUG-FACILITATED SEXUAL ASSAULTS

Drug-Facilitated Sexual Assault (**DFSA**) is an offender's use of "anesthesia-type" drugs or hallucinogens, whether given stealthily or not, to render a subject physically helpless or otherwise incapacitated and thus incapable of giving or withholding consent. Voluntary intoxication does NOT equal consent to have sex, though it does represent risky behavior and leave the person more vulnerable to assault. The various drugs used in DFSA have a variety of effects with the most prevalent being intoxication, amnesia, sleepiness or unconsciousness, and general inability to control their environment. The victim may be unconscious during all or part of act, and may have amnesia even when conscious and appearing to function and "participate" at some stages.

More than 40 different drugs have been used to facilitate sexual assault (and may also be used in robbery). Predatory drugs include these types of drugs:

- Alcohol
- GHB or its "analogs" GBL, BD and others
- Benzodiazepines, such as flunitrazepam (roofies, Rohypnol), Ativan, Xanax, etc.
- Other sedative-hypnotics, such as ketamine, PCP
- Sleeping pills, such as Ambien
- Muscle relaxants, such as Soma, Flexeril
- Antihistamines, such as diphenhydramine (as in Benadryl)
- Animal tranquilizers, such telazol
- Motion sickness/nausea prevention pills, such as scopalomine
- Narcotic analgesics
- MDMA & other hallucinogens

Urine is the sample of choice in DFSA cases and should be obtained as soon as possible, as some of these drugs dissipate from the body rapidly. GHB, for example, is in the blood for only four hours and in the urine for only 12.

Absence of a drug in toxicology results alone does not mean that a drug rape has not occurred. Consider the timing of the event—the time from the suspected drink or food and the time when the sample was finally obtained. A negative toxicology result may merely reflect that the sample was taken after the drug dissipated. The victim's statements, observations by witnesses, etc., may help to establish that a drug, and which drug type, was likely used. Some state laws do not require a positive test result proving a specific drug but may be prosecuted based on effects, observed symptoms, etc. Screening tests may NOT detect all drugs. Confirmation testing should be done when circumstances indicate a possible DFSA and the drug screen is negative.

DRUG STATISTICS

DEA Drug Seizures					
Calender Year	Cocaine kgs	Heroin kgs	Marijuana kgs	Meth kgs	Hallucinogen dosage units
2005	118,270	639	282,139	2,148.6	8,861,503
2004	117,847	672	265,810	1,653.5	2,483,702
2003	73,718	789	254,241	1,676.9	2,879,543
2002	63,640	710	238,646	1,352.8	11,661,811
2001	59,428	753	271,918	1,634.1	13,769,190
2000	58,674	546	331,499	1,771.4	29,307,721
1999	36,165	351	338,287	1,488.8	1,736,118
1998	34,448	371	262,244	1,202.7	1,075,457
1997	28,670	399	215,424	1,143.2	1,100,912
1996	44,735	320	192,132	751.0	1,720,153
1995	45,327	877	219,830	875.1	2,774,376
1994	74,850	491	157,203	767.6	1,367,679
1993	55,655	616	143,056	559.8	2,710,063
1992	69,324	722	201,513	352.7	1,305,208
1991	67,002	1,174	98,620	289.6	1,297,395
1990	60,932	541	133,672	274.5	2,826,966
1989	73,562	758	286,372	896.0	13,125,010
1988	60,951	728	347,306	693.8	16,706,442
1987	49,683	515	629,860	198.6	6,559,317
1986	29,389	421	491,831	234.5	4,146,329

Source: DEA (STRIDE)

DEA Arrests (Domestic)	
Calendar Year	Number of Arrest
2005	28,828
2004	29,952
2003	28,549
2002	30,270
2001	34,471
2000	39,743
1999	41,293
1998	38,468
1997	34,068
1996	29,269
1995	25,279

DEA Arrests (Domestic)	
1994	23,135
1993	21,637
1992	24,541
1991	23,659

Source: DEA (SMARTS)
Defendant Statistical System (DSS)

Heroin Related Emergency Room Visits	
1990	33,884
1991	35,898
1992	48,003
1993	63,232
1994	64,013
1995	70,838
1996	73,846
1997	72,010
1998	77,645
1999	84,409
2000	97,287

Source: Drug Abuse Warning Network)

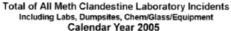

Total of All Meth Clandestine Laboratory Incidents
Including Labs, Dumpsites, Chem/Glass/Equipment
Calendar Year 2005

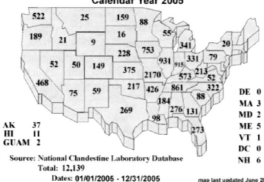

DE	0
MA	3
MD	2
ME	5
VT	1
DC	0
NH	6

AK 37
HI 11
GUAM 2

Source: National Clandestine Laboratory Database
Total: 12,139
Dates: 01/01/2005 - 12/31/2005

map last updated June 2006

Drug Enforcement Administration Heroin Signature Program
The DEA operates the Heroin Signature Program (HSP), using scientific profiling to identify the origin of heroin seized and purchased in the United States. DEA chemists can determine which of the world's four major heroin producing regions was the source of the drug. These regions are: South America, Mexico, Southeast Asia and Southwest Asia. HSP data is used in conjunction with investigative intelligence and with production and seizure data to develop an overall assessment of heroin trafficking to and within the United States. More information is available at the DEA website: **www.dea.gov.**

EARLY WARNING SIGNS

EARLY WARNING SIGNS OF ADOLESCENT DRUG ABUSE

There are numerous early warning signs of adolescent drug abuse. In order to detect the early warning signs, keep an open line of communication and be aware, observant, and open-minded. Drug abuse infiltrates all social, economic, and cultural structures. The current national average of the onset of drug and alcohol use is under 13 years of age.

EARLY WARNING SIGNS:

1. A distinctive change in attitude, usually a negative change.
2. Decline in school work and grades.
3. Poor school attendance, frequent Monday and Friday absences.
4. Distinctive change in friends.
5. Distinctive change in clothing.
6. Distinctive change in tast of music and movies.
7. Disciplinary problems a home and school.
8. Isolation from friends.
9. Mood swings.
10. Outbursts of violence (physical and/or verbal).
11. Discovery of drugs, drug paraphernalia, or drug publications.
12. Distinctive change in appearance. (Examples: tattoos, ear rings, nose rings, etc.)
13. Noticeable decrease in motivation and enthusiasm.
14. Abandonment of areas of interest or hobbies.
15. Stealing (inside and outside the home).
16. Marked increase of physical illness.

GATEWAY DRUGS

Gateway drugs are most commonly used by adolescents. These drugs are:

- Alcohol
- Tobacco (including smokeless)
- Inhalants

Adolescence is the life-stage between childhood and adulthood. The onset of Gateway Drug use was considered to be around age 12 but is often younger. Adolescents use the so-called Gateway Drugs due to the fact they are readily available and inexpensive. These chemicals can cause inhibition of growth and abnormal emotional development. They reason they are called Gateway Drugs is that they can lead the adolescent down the path toward other illicit drug abuse.

More recently MDMA (Ecstasy) has become a major gateway drug and rave parties are often a "gateway event" for the young. The first drug they are exposed to—whatever drug that is—may be the gateway, opening the door to other drug exposure and usage. Parents may serve as the gateway, especially with alcohol, tobacco and today with methamphetamine.

DRUG EVALUATION & TESTING

DRUG EVALUATION

PUPIL/LIGHT ACCOMMODATION TEST

The purpose of this series of tests is to examine the reaction, or lack of reaction, to the presence and absence of light. Use a pen light and a Pupilometer. (Average pupil size is 3.0 to 6.5 millimeters.)

AVAILABLE LIGHT

Using whatever light is available at the time of the test, use a Pupilometer to check the size of both pupils. Always check the left pupil first (to keep the test standardized and systematic) and note the size of each pupil separately. To do this, place the Pupilometer along the temple side of the eye. Locate the circle that best matches the size of the pupil and note that size. (Do not cover any portion of the eye with the Pupilometer during this test.)

CLOSE TO TOTAL DARKNESS

Expose the subject's eyes to a minimum of 90 seconds of uninterrupted, total darkness. Next, place the pad of the index finger over the lens of the pen light. (This will result in a red light.) Place the Pupilometer on the temple side of the eye and shine the red light into the eye. Measure the size of the pupil, doing the left eye first (to keep the test standardized and systematic), then note the size of each pupil separately.

INDIRECT LIGHT

Using the white light of the pen light, illuminate the temple about 6 inches away from the side of the head. Bring inner beam of light forward until it shines across the front of eyeball, creating a shadow or silhouette on the side of the nose halfway between the corner of the eye and the bridge of the nose. Place Pupilometer beside the left eye first (to standardize test) and measure the size of the pupil of each eye separately. (Do not shade the light with the Pupilometer.)

DIRECT LIGHT

Shine the inner beam of the pen light directly into the eye. Position the beam of light between the eyebrows and the top of the cheekbone. Hold the light in this position for one minute. Measure the size of the pupil of the left eye first (to standardize test) with the Pupilometer. Note the measurement of each pupil separately.

HORIZONTAL NYSTAGMUS TEST

SMOOTH PURSUIT

While the subject is looking straight ahead, place a stimulus (index finger) 15 inches in front of the tip of the nose and even with the eyebrows. Move the stimulus (index finger) to the subject's left about 45 degrees watching for an involuntary jerking of the eyes. Proceed to move the stimulus (index finger) to the right eye and repeat procedure. Do this twice with each eye. When moving the stimulus (index finger) to the left, check the left eye. When moving the stimulus (index finger) to the right, check the right eye. Move the stimulus (index finger) straight across in front of the subject's face.

MAXIMUM DEVIATION

Administer this test in the exact same manner as the Smooth Pursuit Test except at the 45 degrees, hold the stimulus (index finger) still for 5 seconds. Look for involuntary jerking of the eye.

NOTE: Some people have nystagmus naturally.

VERTICAL NYSTAGMUS TEST

With the subject looking straight ahead, place the stimulus (index finger) 15 inches out from the tip of the nose. Move stimulus (index finger) upward level with the top of the head and down to the tip of the nose. Do this test at least twice looking at each eye once. Record your results.

NOTE Vertical Nystagmus is when the eyeballs jerk vertically (up and down).

NON-CONVERGENCE TEST

When the subject is looking straight ahead, place the stimulus (index finger) 15 inches in front of the tip of the nose. First move the stimulus in front of the face counter clockwise. The circles should not be larger than the subject's face.

When you are sure the subject is following the stimulus with his eyes, bring the stimulus (index finger) to the nose and touch the bridge of the nose. Tell the subject to watch the stimulus (index finger) on the bridge of the nose for at least 5 seconds. Look for either or both eyes drifting outward, not being able to focus inward on the nose.

NOTE: Non-convergence can be natural in some individuals.

STANDARD FIELD SOBRIETY TESTS

The following is an explanation of the four standardized field sobriety tests. Please keep in mind:

1. These tests should be used for **ALL** drug influence situations, not just for alcohol intoxication.

2. Give clear instructions to the subject and be sure they understand what is required of them before they begin each test.

3. Conduct each test on a flat surface that is well-lighted and void of any obstructions.

4. Discontinue any test if the subject is in any danger of injury.

5. Take complete notes as you administer each test.

6. These tests should be given in the same order and instructed in the same way each time to standardize the tests.

RHOMBERG 30 SECOND ESTIMATION OF TIME

During the explanation and demonstration of this test, have the subject stand upright with heels and toes together and their hands at their sides. This is the "Rhomberg Position."

TEST: In the "Rhomberg Position," have the subject tilt his head back and close his eyes. When you say begin, have the subject estimate 30 seconds. (This should be done silently.) When the subject believes the 30 seconds are finished, he should open his eyes and bring his head forward. This indicates the end of the test. If the subject has not completed the test in 90 seconds, discontinue the test.

NOTES

1. Drugs that speed up the body will cause a short estimation of time (Cocaine, amphetamines, etc.), and the drugs that slow the system down will cause a long estimation of time (depressants, narcotics, alcohol, etc.).

2. Be aware of the actual time during the test. Note body movements such as swaying, body tremors, muscle rigidity, etc.

3. Make sure the subject performs the test as instructed.

WALK AND TURN

During the explanation and demonstration, have the subject place his right foot on the line he will be walking on. Then have him place the toes of his left foot against the heel of his right foot. Standing flat on the ground with both feet pointing in the same direction, stand up straight with both arms at his side.

TEST: After assuming the above position, instruct the subject to walk nine steps up the line, turn around and walk nine steps back. (Each step should be heel to toe.) The subject will look down at his feet and count each step out loud. At the end of the first nine steps, the subject will turn. (The turn will be a three-point pivot), keeping the front foot in its place and using the balls of this foot to pivot.) With the back foot, push three times around to face the opposite direction. Walk back nine steps in the same manner. If at any time the subject falls off the line, he is to regain his balance and continue to walk and count off his steps where he left off. Discontinue test if subject is in danger of injury.

NOTES

1. Note any difficulties balancing.
2. Note if the subject uses his arms or any other object for balance.
3. Be sure he touches heel to toe as instructed.
4. Make sure the turn is done as instructed.
5. The counting of steps should be loud enough to be heard.
6. Make sure the subject performs the test as instructed.

ONE LEG STAND

During the explanation and demonstration, have the subject stand in the "Rhomberg Position." (Stand upright with heels and toes together, and hands at the side.)

TEST: From the "Rhomberg Position," instruct the subject to first balance on his left leg by raising his right leg until his right foot is six inches off the ground. Have the subject point his toes down on the right foot, and while looking at his right foot, count to 30 out loud. (Have the subject count one thousand one, one thousand two, one thousand three, etc.) If at any time the subject loses his balance, he is to regain balance and continue counting where he left off. Discontinue test if subject is in danger of injury.

NOTES

1. Note if subject uses arms or any other object for balance.
2. Note any difficulties in balancing.
3. The subject must count correctly.
4. Make sure the subject performs the test as instructed.

FINGER TO THE NOSE

During the explanation and demonstration, the subject should stand in the "Rhomberg Position." (Stand upright with heels and toes together, and hands at the side.) Have the subject make a fist with both hands and extend his index finger on each hand, then place his arms at his sides.

TEST: From the above position, instruct the subject to tilt his head back and close his eyes. When instructed, the subject is to touch the tip of his index finger to the tip of his nose. After touching his nose, the subject will bring his hand down to the starting position without being told. The sequence of instruction is left, right, left, right, right, left.

NOTES

1. Note any body movements, such as swaying, body tremors, muscle rigidity, etc.

2. Observe where the index finger touches the face.

3. Make sure the subject performs the test as instructed.

DRUG TESTING

BODY FLUIDS REQUIRED FOR TESTING

Choice of body fluid will depend on a variety of considerations, including the drug that is suspected and the timing of when the sample is being taken. With alcohol, blood or breath is preferred. If, however, other drugs are involved, urine may be preferred. If the suspect is clearly under the influence, blood may be an appropriate choice, as in drunk/drugged driving cases where the subject is still under the influence at the time the sample is taken. With possible drug-facilitated sexual assault cases, urine is always the preferred sample. If collection is being made within a few hours of the suspected drugging, blood may be worthwhile, and could be taken in addition to a urine sample.

Blood and urine have both advantages and disadvantages. The presence of drugs in blood is more closely related to impairment, but may be more difficult to obtain (requiring specially trained personnel) and is often more expensive to analyze. Urine is easier to obtain and the concentration of drugs and metabolites in urine is often easier to detect. Drugs remain in urine longer than in blood. Taking urine specimens may allow the subject a greater opportunity to tamper with the sample contents (adding someone else's urine, diluting the sample, etc,).

UNDERSTANDING TOXICOLOGY RESULTS

Toxicology results can be confusing as they may be reported in a variety of concentration units. They may be reported as nanograms per milliliter (ng/mL). Other labs use micrograms per milliliter (μg/mL). There is a 1,000-time difference between nanograms and micrograms, making comparison and understand very confusing.

UNITS OF CONCENTRATION CONVERSION

1 mg/L	=	1 μg/mL
1 mg/mL	=	1000 ug/mL
1 μg/mL	=	1000 ng/mL
1 mg/dL	=	10 μg/mL
100 μg/dL	=	1 μg/mL

DETECTION LIMITS

Note: Times relate to length of time drugs can be detected in urine, except where blood limitations are specifically noted. Times are estimates and specific drugs within categories may vary.

Cocaine . . . . 2-3 days
Metabolite*

Cannabis
Single use . . . . 3 days
Moderate use (4 times/week) . . . . 5 days
Heavy use (daily) . . . . 10 days
Chronic heavy use . . . . 21-27 days

Gamma Hydroxybutyrate (GHB & Analogs GBL & BD)
Urine . . . . 12 hours
Blood . . . . 3-5 hours

Opiates . . . . 48 hours
(including heroin, morphine, codeine)

PCP (Phencyclidine) . . . 48 hours to 8 days

Amphetamines . . . . 48 hours
(including methamphetamines)

Benzodiazepines** . . . . 3 days, approx
(including diazepam/Valium, clonazepam/Klonopins, therapeutic dose)

Barbiturates
Short acting (secobarbital) . . . . 24 hours
Intermediate acting . . . . 48-72 hours
Long acting (phenobarbital) . . 7 days or more
Phenobarbital . . . . 24 hours (blood)

Propoxyphene (Darvon)
Unchanged . . . . 6 hours
Metabolite* . . . . 6-48 hours

*A metabolite is the substance(s) produced by the body metabolizing (breaking down) a drug. Metabolites may by psychoactive or inactive, but are detectable in blood and urine and are often the basis for drug tests. For example, cocaine produces the metabolite benzoylecogonine; when cocaethylene (aka ethylcocaine) is detected, that indicates combined use of alcohol and cocaine. Presence of the parent drug, cocaine, indicates recent use. Some drugs are detected only as the drug itself, with no metabolites, such as PCP.

**There is a wide range of benzodiazepine drugs available and some may not be readily detectable in a "drug screen" (i.e. immunoassay) in either blood or urine, such as lorazepam (Ativan), alprazolam (Xanax) and triazolam (Halcion). Other testing procedures should be used before ruling out the presence of benzos.

WEIGHTS & MEASURES

DRY MEASURES

1 Microgram (mcg.)	=	1/1000 of a Milligram (mg.)
1000 Micrograms (mcg.)	=	1 Milligram (mg.)
1000 Grams	=	1 Kilogram (kilo.)
1 Kilogram (kilo.)	=	2.2 Pounds (lbs.)
1 Gram (g.)	=	15.43 Grains (gr.)
28.35 Grams (g.)	=	1 Ounce (oz.)
453.6 Grams (g.)	=	1 Pound (lb.)
1 Grain (gr.)	=	65 Milligrams (mg.)
1 Grain (gr.)	=	.065 Grams (g.)
1 Ounce (oz.)	=	437.5 Grains (gr.)
1 Ounce (oz.)	=	28.3 Grams (g.)
1 Ounce (oz.)	=	28,350 Milligrams (mg.)
1 Ounce (oz.)	=	6 Tablespoons (tbls.) approx.
1 Pound (lbs.)	=	7,000 Grains
1 Pound (lbs.)	=	16 Ounces
1 Pound (lbs.)	=	453 Grams (g.)
1 Ton	=	2,000 Pounds (lbs.)

LIQUID MEASURES

1 L (Liter)	=	approximately one quart
1000ml (milliliters)	=	1 Liter

NOTE: For comparison purposes and for training, one gram equals one packet of sugar substitute, such as Sweet N Low.

WORKPLACE DRUG ABUSE

STATISTICS:

1. An estimated 70% of all individuals abusing drugs are employed.

2. The abuse of alcohol and other drugs is costing American business owners over one hundred billion ($100,000,000, 000) dollars annually due to insurance rate increases, workman's compensation, etc.

3. Drug use shows up at all levels in the workplace, from professionals to unskilled workers.

4. An estimated 20% of the workplace population is using alcohol or other drugs at the workplace.

5. Almost 60% of the worlds production of illegal drugs are consumed in the United States while only 5% of the world's population is located in the United States.

ABUSERS IN THE WORKPLACE:

1. Are less productive.

2. Miss several days of work.

3. Are more likely to injure themselves or someone else.

4. File more worker's compensation claims.

5. Are more likely to steal from employer and/or co-workers.

6. A cause of low morale among co-workers.

7. Cause an increase in co-worker's work load.

8. Cause insurance rates to increase.

RECOGNIZING ABUSERS IN THE WORKPLACE:

1. Accidents on the job.

2. Frequent absences and/or late to work.

3. Frequent mistakes that require additional work to correct.

4. Uncharacteristic behavior (moodiness, giddiness, violent threats, etc.).

5. Obsessed with drugs and alcohol and trying to get others to participate.

FIGHTING WORKPLACE DRUG ABUSE - FIVE PART PROGRAM:

1. A written substance abuse policy.

2. An employee education & awareness program.

3. Supervisor training program.

4. An employee assistance program.

5. Drug testing when appropriate.

RESOURCES FOR
WORKPLACE DRUG ABUSE

California Narcotic Officers' Association
1(877) 775-6272
www.cnoa.org

American Council for Drug Education
1(800) 488-DRUG (3784)
1(301) 394-0600

Drug-Free Workplace Helpline
1(800) 843-4971 (9am to 8 pm EST)
1(800) WORKPLACE
www.health.org/workpl.htm

National Clearinghouse for Alcohol & Drug Information
1(800) 729-6686

National Institute on Drug Abuse Treatment (NIDA) Hotline
1(800) 662-HELP (4357)

The Resource Center for Alcohol and Drug Problems
1(800) 879-2772

SAMHSA Treatment Facilities Locator
http://dasis3.samhsa.gov/

Resources for Drug Prevention

www.projectghb.org
www.taylorhooton.org
www.couragetospeak.org
www.notMYkid.org
www.dammad.org
www.painfullyobvious.com
www.teens.drugabuse.gov
www.theantidrug.com
www.drugfree.org
www.justthinktwice.com

STREET SLANG GLOSSARY

DEFINITIONS & STREET SLANG GLOSSARY

DEFINITIONS

ANABOLIC STEROID   Medically used to some extent but also personally abused to promote muscle growth and tissue development. Typically abused by athletes but increased use has been seen among teens to overcome harassment for being small, skinny and by young females to be more firm and lean. Users run the risk of increased cancer, acne and other negative side effects. Many counterfeit products are also being distributed.

ANALGESIC   Drugs that relieve pain, such as codeine, zolpidem, oxycodone, etc.

ANALOG   Chemical cousin of another drug, with similar properties and related chemical structure (definition for legal purposes varies from state to state). This is the basis for "designer drug" issues, where a chemist may alter the structure of an illegal substance, seeking a drug of similar properties for abuse purposes but not yet illegal. But, when and where analog laws apply (and depending on the precise wording), the new substance may be automatically covered and made illegal for human consumption.

ATAXIA   Loss of muscle coordination.

CNS   Central Nervous System.

CNS   Central Nervous System.

HYPERTHERMIA   Over-heating of the body due to certain drug effects or disease. Defined as body temperature over 104 degrees. Drugs associated with this include MDMA, LSD, amphetamines, cocaine, PCP, etc.

HYPOTHERMIA   Decreased body temperature due to exposure to cold, certain drug effects. Defined as body temperature below 90 degrees. Drugs associated with this include barbiturates, ethanol, GHB, sedative-hypnotics, opiates, etc.

SINSEMILLA   Seedless marijuana.

SYNESTHESIA   The effect of drugs such as LSD in which the user's sensory system is crossed, resulting in the "seeing" sounds, "hearing" colors, etc.

TACHYCARDIA   Excessive heart rate (pulse greater than 100).

STREET SLANG

Street slang varies from city to city, state to state, culture
to culture, etc. We have attempted to gather
the most commonly used terms.

2-CI   Emerging street drug 2,5-dimethoxy-4-iodophenethy-
lamine (See TRYPTAMINE)

2-CB   Street drug 4-bromo-2,5-dimethoxyphenethylamine (see
NEXUS, BROMO)

2C-T-7   Street drug 2,5-dimethoxy-4-(n)-propylthiophenethyl-
amine known as Tripstasy, Lucky 7, 7-Up (See LUCKY 7)

8-TRACK   Street gang term meaning 2.5 grams of Cocaine

ABE   Five dollars worth of a drug

ABSINTHE   An alcoholic beverage with serious side effects
that was notoriously popular with artists like Vincent van Gogh;
contains thujone, a sedating substance from the plant Artemisia
absinthium, also called wormwood; renewed interest in this
substance has surfaced in recent years despite the risk of
psychosis

ACAPULCO GOLD   A particularly potent form of Marijuana
grown in the Acapulco area (See GOLD and GOLD LEAF)

ACCESSORIES   Drug paraphernalia

ACE   1) A Marijuana cigarette (See JOINT) **2)** P.C.P.

ACETONE   A chemical that is mainstay of many illicit drug
preparations, making it a regulated chemical; can also be
abused as an inhalant

ACID   L.S.D. (Lysergic Acid Diethylamide) ACID CUBE A sugar
cube containing L.S.D.

ACID FREAK   A heavy regular user of L.S.D.

ACID HEAD   L.S.D. user

ACK-ACK   Method by which Heroin/Cocaine is smoked on the
tip of a burning cigarette ACTION To use or sell drugs AD A drug
addict

ADAM   Slang for the drug MDMA (3,4-Methylenedioxy-N-
Methylamphetamine)

ADAM & EVE IN THE GARDEN OF EDEN   Polydrug abuse,
called a flip, taking MDMA with the drugs MDEA and MBDB, all
at the same time (See FLIP)

AFGHANI   Drugs from Afghanistan Usually Marijuana

AMF   Slang for the drug Alpha-Methylfentanyl

AMPED   High on amphetamines

AMBIEN Sleeping pill containing Zolpidem that can be abused or used for drugging for rape or robbery

AMT/a-MT Alpha-methyl-tryptamine is another drug being seen in pill or powder form, typically in same clientele as MDMA; also called Spirals, Amtrak or Amthrax (See TRYPTAMINE)

AMYL NITRATE A prescription drug for coronary artery disease that is also abused by inhaling the fumes, giving a brief but intense rush (See POPPERS, BUTYL NITRATE)

ANABOLIC STEROID Medically used to some extent but also personally abused to promote muscle growth and tissue development; typically abused by athletes but increased use has been seen among teens to overcome harassment for being small, skinny and by young females to be more firm and lean; users run the risk of increased cancer, acne and other negative side effects; many counterfeit products are also being distributed

ANALGESIC Drugs that relieve pain, such as codeine, zolpidem, oxycodone, etc.

ANALOG Chemical cousin of another drug, with similar properties and related chemical structure (definition for legal purposes varies from state to state); this is the basis for "designer drug" issues, where a chemist may alter the structure of an illegal substance, seeking a drug of similar properties for abuse purposes but not yet illegal; when and where analog laws apply (and depending on the precise wording), the new substance may be automatically covered and made illegal for human consumption

ANGEL DUST 1) Phencyclidine (P.C.P.) **2)** P.C.P. sprinkled on Marijuana in powdered form and smoked

ANGEL'S TRUMPET The Datura plant, a hallucinogen, is also called Angel's Trumpet or Devil Weed or Jimson Weed (See DATURA)

ANIMAL TRANK P.C.P.

ARTILLERY Drug paraphernalia for injecting

ASTRO TURF Marijuana

ATROPINE From datura and belladonna plants, atropine has legitimate medical uses but abuse can produce hallucinations, severe toxic effects and even death

AUTHOR A doctor or anyone who writes illegal prescriptions

BABYSITTER An individual knowledgeable about the effects of hallucinogens, particularly in the case of L.S.D. The babysitter provides reassurance and reality for the novice user (See CO-PILOT)

BACK-UP A procedure permitting blood back into the syringe to ensure that the needle is in a vein (a frequent precaution taken by veteran heroin addicts)

BAD TRIP An unpleasant, frightening or even terrifying experience occurring after the ingestion of a hallucinogenic drug or after ingestion of other drugs with hallucinogenic properties

BAG A small container of a drug, usually just enough for personal use

BALL Mexican Black Tar Heroin

BALLOON A toy balloon used for packaging Mexican Powdered Heroin. The balloon is used to enable the possessor to swallow it if approached by the authorities. It is later retrieved after defecation

BANG Injecting

BARBS Barbiturates

BARREL 1) A quantity of 100,000 pills 2) A particular shape of L.S.D. tablet

BASA Spanish word for base

BASE Freebased Cocaine

BASEBALL Cocaine Freebase

BASINE The process of converting powdered Cocaine (Hydrochloride) into a purified solid for smoking

BASUCO/BASA Raw Coca Paste directly from the Coca Plant. It is a dark paste that is smoked, usually by South American peasants

BATU Hawaiian term for the large smokable crystals of Methamphetamine

BAYONET Hypodermic syringe

BC Bud Marijuana from British Columbia

BEANS 1)Dexedrine; 2) more currently and commonly used to refer to MDMA pills, especially in Florida

BEAUTIFUL A drug of good quality, producing an exceptionally intense euphoria

BEHIND STUFF Using heroin, as in "I'm behind stuff"

BELLY HABIT Addiction where withdrawals cause severe stomach cramps

BELT 1) High or Euphoria produced by a drug high; 2) To quickly consume alcohol;3) A large mouthful of alcohol.

BENNIES The prescription drug Benzedrine, however, it is no longer manufactured (See BENZ and DRIVERS)

BENT To be high on any drug

BENZ The prescription drug Benzedrine, however, it is no longer manufactured (See BENNIES and DRIVERS)

BENZODIAZEPINE (aka BENZO) A group of depressant drugs typically for sleep or anxiety disorders, such as Valium, Xanax, Ativan (See depressants)

BERNICE Cocaine

BETEL NUT From the areca palm tree, betel nut is commonly used in some Asian cultures and produces a mild stimulant effect

BHANG Marijuana

BIG CHIEF Peyote

BIG C Cocaine

BIG D L.S.D.

BIG H Heroin

BIG MAN Upper level drug dealer

BINDLE Paper used to hold a personal amount of a powdered drug Folded like an envelope

BINGE A sustained period of uninterrupted alcohol uses, sometimes refers to the same practice with other drugs

BINKY or BINKIE Pacifiers used by abusers of the drug MDMA (Ecstasy) to reduce the bruxism (teeth grinding) that it often causes

BLACK & WHITES Biphetamine that comes in a black & white capsule (See BLACK BEAUTIES)

BLACK BEAUTIES Biphetamine that comes in a black and white capsule (See BLACK & WHITES)

BLACK JACK Tincture of Opium cooked to a concentrated form and injected

BLACK TAR HEROIN A form of Mexican Heroin

BLANK An inert substance mixed with a drug to produce more of the substance for sales

BLASTED An intense drug high

BLAZING Smoking marijuana

BLOND Gold or yellow colored solid Hashish from the Middle East (Lebanese Blond)

BLOTTER ACID Small squares of heavy stock paper, perforated for tearing, with a drop of L.S.D. on each. Ingested orally. Sometimes there are pictures stamped on each one.

BLOW 1) Slang for Cocaine; 2) Inhalation of smoke

BLOW A STICK (OR JOINT) Smoking a marijuana joint

BLOW THE VEIN Injecting a vein with too much of the substance usually causing the vein to collapse

BLOW YOUR MIND To get high on a hallucinogenic

BLOWING UP (or BLOWIN' UP)   Getting high on MDMA (Ecstasy)

BLUE CHEER   A combination of L.S.D., Methamphetamine, and Strychnine

BLUE DEVILS   Prescription drug Amytal Sodium in a blue capsule

BLUE HEAVEN   L.S.D.

BLUELIGHTER   Refers to someone who participates in the on-line message board called bluelight, a common discussion ground for ravers and drug abusers (www.bluelight.nu)

BLUE MYSTIC   Street drug 2C-T-7, also called Triptasy or 7-Up (See TRYPTAMINE)

BLUE NITRO   Common GBL product (GHB analog) disguised as a dietary supplement

BLUES   Amytal Sodium capsule

BLUE STAR   A type of Morning Glory plant. The seeds can cause hallucinations similar to that of L.S.D.

BLUE VELVET   Tincture of Opium added to powdered Tripelennamine, made into a solution and injected for a very intense high

BLUNT   Hollowed out cigar filled with marijuana

BO   Street gang term for Marijuana

BOAT   1,000 MDMA pills; also called a bucket in some regions

BODY CARRIER   Drug smuggler who carries the contraband in their clothes or on their body

BODY PACKER   Drug smuggler who swallows the contraband which is usually wrapped in balloons or condoms. Later it is retrieved after defecation (see MULE)

BOGART   Not sharing any drug

BOMBED   Excessive drug intoxication

BOLIVIAN   1) Cocaine of the purest form; 2) Country of origin

BOLSA   Spanish word for bag. Usually refers to Heroin

BOLT   Amyl Nitrite

BONG   Marijuana smoking pipe that is usually glass with a cooling chamber that is filled with water or wine

BOWL   1) Marijuana pipe; 2) A degree measurement of Marijuana

BOTTLE   100 pills

BOY   Heroin

BRICK   A quantity of Marijuana compressed into the shape of a brick that usually weighs a kilogram (2.2 lbs.)

BRING DOWN 1) To precipitate a "crash" from the excessive agitation produced by stimulants, via the ingestion of a CNS depressant; **2)** To help reduce highly adverse effects produced in some h hallucinogen users via talk, reassurance, and sometimes minor tranquilizers

BRING IT UP To bulge a vein prior to injection

BRODY, TO THROW A To feign illness or withdraw in an attempt to obtain a narcotic prescription from a sympathetic physician

BROTHER Heroin

BROWN STUFF Mexican Brown Powdered Heroin

BROWNIES Regular fudge brownies mixed with Marijuana

BRUXISM Teeth grinding and jaw locking commonly caused by drugs such as MDMA and methamphetamine

BUCKET 1,000 MDMA pills in some regions; more commonly called a boat (See BOAT)

BUD The blossom at the top of the Marijuana plant that contains the highest level of THC which is the active component of the plant

BUDDHA STICK Potent Asian Marijuana which is wrapped around bamboo sticks for shipping

BUFF/BUFFED 1) To dilute a drug;**2)** Muscular in appearance from use of steroids and/or exercise

BUG Itching sensation, due to cocaine overdose BUGGER Black Tar Heroin

BULLET 1) Bullet-shaped plastic tube used for snorting drugs in the powdered form;**2)** One year jail term

BUMMED/BUMMER 1) Bad trip;**2)** A bad experience not necessarily drug related

BUMP (aka LINE) 1) Refers to a line, a bump or pile of cocaine, meth, MDMA or ketamine powder to be snorted, usually 0.2 grams per line; **2)** Internet jargon on message boards for agreeing with the last person/message

BUM TRIP A bad hallucinogenic drug experience

BUNK Low grade drug. Often the adulterant is solo and being represented as the drug

BURN Substances used to dilute potency of drug such as lidocaine, procaine, nicotinamide, or ephedrine

BURNED Cheated by a drug dealer

BURNED OUT In a state of brain or chronic behavior impairment resulting from chronic heavy drug use.

BUSH Marijuana

BUSINESSMAN'S LUNCH DMT, a hallucinogen with potent effects lasting 30-60 minutes

BUST An arrest by authorities and confiscation of drugs

BUTTON The top middle flower area of the Peyote Cactus (Hemispheric Taberculous). A hard, round object, slightly larger than a golf ball, containing the active ingredient of the plant, Mescaline, a hallucinogen

BUTYL NITRATE A chemical abused by inhalation for the intense rush it provides; was sold over the counter in small vials as incense, cleaner, etc.; may still be diverted from legitimate chemical use

BUY A drug purchase

BUZZ A drug high

BZP In medical notes may refer to benzodiazepine but in the street refers to BENZYLPIPERAZINE, another drug abused by MDMA users for the related effects (See also TFMPP or MOLLY)

C Cocaine

C&H Cocaine and Heroin

CABALLO Spanish word for Heroin

CACTUS Peyote Cactus

CADET First time drug user

CALIFORNIA SUNSHINE L.S.D. produced and sold on the West Coast of California

CAMEL Drug smuggler or drug carrier

CAN One ounce quantity of Marijuana

CANDY Cocaine or MDMA

CANDY FLIP Refers to the polydrug "flip" of taking both MDMA and LSD; users are encouraged to take the LSD about three hours before taking Ecstasy (See FLIP)

CANDY MAN Drug dealer or drug supplier

CANDY RAVER Rave attendee who dresses in infantile garb, wears bead/candy necklaces and pacifiers and takes the drug MDMA (Ecstasy) (See RAVE)

CAP 1) Powdered drug in capsule form; 2) GHB users typically dose in caps, measured by water bottle caps, for example, which is about 6-7 ml

CAP-UP To put powdered drugs into capsules

CARGA Spanish word for Heroin

CARRIER Drug smuggler or transporter

CARTWHEELS White Amphetamine tablets

CAT 1) Heroin; 2) A synthetic designer drug, methcathinone, a stimulant with no medical application

CAT VALIUM The drug ketamine, primarily used as a small animal anesthetic but also has use in pediatrics and as a battlefield anesthetic

CATHINONE and CATHINE The leaves of the Khat (or catha edulis) plant common to locations such as Somolia, often chewed for the stimulant effect; when fresh, the leaves contain cathinone, a Schedule I substance, but once dried, the substance deteriorates to the weaker version, cathine, which is on Schedule IV

CCC Refers to the brand "Coricidin Cough & Cold" tablets containing dextromethorphan (DXM), widely abused by teens who take from 10 to 45 pills at a time (See also RED DEVILS, TRIPLE C, THE MATRIX, DXM)

CECIL/CEC Cocaine

CHANNEL Vein used for injecting drugs

CENT One dollar

CHAPAPOTE Spanish word for Mexican Tar Heroin

CHARAS Hindu for Marijuana

CHARGE The first effect of a drug high

CHARLIE Cocaine

CHASING THE DRAGON Heating Heroin or Opium on a piece of foil and inhaling the smoke

CHINA WHITE **1)** Southeastern Asian Heroin;**2)** The synthetic opiate Alpha-Methylfentanyl

CHIPPER/TO CHIP **1)** An occasional drug user;**2)** To inject just under the skin

CHIPPING Taking narcotic analgesics on an occasional or irregular basis, not sufficiently often enough to become physically dependent

CHIVA Spanish word for Heroin

CHOKING GAME A method of self-asphyxiation by cutting off the supply of oxygen/blood flow to the brain by pressing the thumbs against the carotid artery for the high or rush it gives and causing the person to pass out briefly, fall limp and thus release the flow of blood; this game has been around for years but has reached higher risk levels by involving others as the choker and utilizing belts or other props, increasing the risk that airflow or blood flow would be withheld too long, causing brain damage or death; participants are often young teens

CHOPPING To dilute or adulterate a drug

CHRISTMAS TREES The prescription drug Tuinal

CHRONIC High grade marijuana

CIRCLES Rohypnol

CLEAN Drug free

CLENBUTEROL Abused by some bodybuilders/athletes for alleged fat burning, stimulant and muscle enhancing effects, despite negative side effects

CLUB DRUGS Common term for a variety of drugs used in rave and nightclub scene, loosely including MDMA (Ecstasy), LSD, ketamine, GHB, meth, marijuana and other hallucinogens

CLUCK HEAD Street gang term for Cocaine addict

COASTING The euphoric high just after taking a drug, usually associated with Heroin

COAST TO COASTS Amphetamine tablets

COCAINE BLUES Depression from discontinuing use of cocaine

COKE Cocaine

COKE BUGS The sensation of bugs crawling under or on the user's skin associated with a Cocaine overdose

COKE HEAD A Cocaine user

COKE SPOON A small metal spoon used for snorting (inhaling) Cocaine

COKED OUT Excessive use of cocaine to point of incoherence

COKED UP Label for erratic behavior due to excessive use of cocaine

COLA Cocaine

COLD TURKEY Abrupt withdrawal from long term drug abuse

COLUM Street gang term used for Colombian Marijuana

COME DOWN The gradual wearing-off of the effects of drugs

COME-ON The first feeling after taking a drug

COMMERCIAL Street gang term used for Marijuana

CONNECT/CONNECTION Drug dealer or supplier

CONTACT HIGH Mild euphoria occurring in non-smokers and believed by them to be the result of inhalation of the Marijuana fumes produced by smokers

COOK To prepare or heat a drug into liquid form in preparation for injection

COOKED High on drugs

COOKER **1)** The container in which drugs are heated for injection. For example: Spoons, bottle caps, bottom half of a soft drink or beer can, etc.;**2)** One who manufactures drugs in a lab

COOKIE Chunk of rock cocaine

COOKING COTTONS When a Heroin addict can not get Heroin, he will use the old cotton

COP   To purchase drugs

CO-PILOT   An individual knowledgeable about the effects of hallucinogens, particularly in the case of L.S.D. The Co-Pilot provides reassurance and reality for the novice user (See BABYSITTER)

CORINE   Cocaine

COTTON   A small amount of cotton used to filter impurities from dissolved Heroin as it is drawn into the hypodermic

COTTON, ASKING FOR   Refers to an impoverished heroin addict to afford a "buy" scrounging the cotton used as a filter by other addicts that a very weak heroin solution can be made

COTTON FEVER   During the process of injecting, a small piece of cotton is used as a filter when the drug, usually Heroin, is drawn up into the syringe. Occasionally a fiber of cotton is drawn up into the syringe and is injected causing the user to become extremely ill

COTTON MOUTH   Dry mouth caused by ingestion of certain drugs

COURIER   Drug smuggler or transporter

CRACK   Cocaine Hydrochloride (powder) that has been processed into a pure solid form for smoking

CRACK HOUSE   A structure where Crack (Freebased Cocaine) is sold

CRACKER   A device used to "crack open" small nitrous oxide cartridges and divert the gas into a balloon for huffing (See NITROUS OXIDE or WHIPPETS)

CRANK   Methamphetamine

CRANKSTER   User of Methamphetamine

CRANK BUGS   The sensation of bugs crawling on or under the user's skin associated with a Methamphetamine overdose

CRAP   **1)** Heroin;**2)** Low quality drug

CRASH   To abruptly stop using a drug

CRATE   A large quantity of pills, usually 50,000

CRATER   A deep flesh indentation at a particular site which has been subjected to repeated intravenous injections

CRINK   Methamphetamine

CROKE   To use Cocaine and Methamphetamine together

CROSS-TOPS   Benzedrine tablets, so name for the crossed lines on one side of the pill as a result of the pill press mold.

CRYSTAL   Methamphetamine

CUBE   A sugar cube containing L.S.D.

CUT   To adulterate or dilute drugs

CYCLING   Using different types of steroids one after another, but not at the same time. Example: Use a particular type of steroid for a period of time then use a different type of steroid to gain the maximum effect and reduce side effects

D   L.S.D.

D & G   MDMA pills with the logo D&G for clothing designers Dolce & Gabanna, one of many business logos used on the illicit pills

DATE RAPE DRUG (RAPE DRUG)   Any drug used to render someone unable to give or withhold consent to sexual activity, such as CNS depressants or hallucinogens (See DFSA)

DATURA   The genus of plants commonly called jimson weed, angel's trumpet, moonflower, devil's weed; leaves, seeds and roots contain atropine, scopolamine and hyoscyamine, three toxic alkaloids; abuse by smoking or making tea to hallucinate can be fatal

DAVA   Heroin

DEAD PRESIDENTS   Street gang term for money

DEAL/DEALER   To sell drugs/One who sells drugs

DEATH   Refers to the drugs PMA and PMMA, similar to MDMA but more intense in effects and have a greater risk of death

DESIGNATED SITTER   Someone who babysits others who are tripping on hallucinogens

DESIGNER DRUG   Drugs designed by chemists as similar to the chemistry and property of other drugs, often to try to sidestep the law if the primary drug is already illegal. Also loosely used interchangeably by some with the term Club Drugs (See ANALOG)

DEVIL DUST   PCP

DEXIES   The prescription stimulant drug Dexedrine

DFSA or DRUG FACILITATED SEXUAL ASSAULT   The use of drugs to render a person unable to give or withhold consent to have sex (See DATE RAPE DRUG)

DIAMONDS   Amphetamine tablets

DILLIES   Dilaudid (Hydromorphine)

DIME   Ten dollars

DIME BAG   Ten dollars worth of a drug

DIRTY   **1)** To possess drugs; **2)** To give a positive body fluid test

DIRTY PEE   Positive urine test

DITCH WEED   Low quality Marijuana

D.M.T. The synthetic hallucinogen Dimethyltryptamine, also called "Businessman's lunch because the effects last less than an hour

DO A LINE To snort (inhale) a "line" of a drug in powder form

DOING CAPS Taking GHB by the capful

DO UP To inject

D.O.A. Dead on arrival

DOB 2,5 dimethyoxy-4-bromoamphetamine, potent hallucinogen, one of many that may be encountered as a substitute for MDMA

DOLLAR One hundred dollars worth of a drug

DOLLY Dolophine (Methadone)

DOOBIE Marijuana cigarette (See JOINT)

DOORS & FOURS Taking the prescription drugs Doriden and Tylenol w/Codeine #4 together. The effects are similar to that of Heroin

DOPE General term for drugs

DOPE FIEND Drug user

DOPER Drug user

DOSE 1) The amount of a drug taken;2) The amount of Methadone, a synthetic narcotic used to treat Heroin addiction, that is taken

DOSING Taking drugs

DOT A dose of L.S.D. so small it is hard to see

DOUBLE STACK An MDMA (Ecstasy) pill that is double thick in size and dosage; also a nickname for the deadly drug PMA that is similar to MDMA but more severe

DOWNER Barbiturates or tranquilizers

DOWN, GET DOWN Inject a drug

DRAGGED A mild anxiety and fatigue state following Marijuana intoxication

DREAMERS Narcotic analgesic drugs

DRIVERS The prescription drug Benzedrine, however, it is no longer manufactured (See BENNIES and BENZ)

DROP To take a drug orally

DROP A TAB To take L.S.D. orally

DROP A DIME To inform on someone

DROPPER Hypodermic syringe

DRUGGIE Drug user

DRY 1) To be drug free;2) When the supply of drugs are low or gone

DRY OUT   To abstain from drugs or alcohol after a prolonged use, to the point of substantial or complete loss of tolerance

DRY UP   When drugs, usually narcotics, are not available

DUCKETS   Street gang term for money

DUST   1) A drug in powder form;2) Cocaine;3) P.C.P. (Phencyclidine)

DUST OFF   A commercial air cleaner for computers, etc., that is being abused as an inhalant (See DUSTING)

DUSTED   Under the influence of P.C.P.

DUSTER   P.C.P. user

DUSTING   1) Combining marijuana and heroin and rolling it in a form to be smoked; 2) Inhaling the spray product DUST OFF

DXM   The cough suppressant dextromethorphan, commonly abused especially by teens; taken in quantities from 300 to 900 milligrams to achieve high and/or hallucinations

DYNO   High quality drug

EASY LAY   The drug gamma hydroxybutyrate, GHB

EAT   To swallow drugs rather than be caught with them

ECHOES   L.S.D. flashbacks

ECSTACY   Refers to ephedrine and herbal products seeking to resemble the drug MDMA in terms of stimulating effects. Note the spelling difference from the drug MDMA's nickname ECSTASY

E/ECSTASY   The synthetic drug M.D.M.A. (3,4-Methylenedioxy-N-Methylamphetamine); See also XTC or X

EIGHT BALL   1/8 ounce of a drug

EIGHTH   1/8 of an ounce or a gram

ELEPHANT   P.C.P. (Phencyclidine)

ELEPHANT FLIP   The polydrug flip of PCP and MDMA

ELEVEN-FIVE-FIFTY   Under the influence of a controlled substance California Health & Safety Code section violation (11550 H&S)

EMBALMING FLUID   An old nickname for PCP but current use also involves the actual abuse of embalming fluid, which contains formaldehyde and gives a similar bizarre behavior state but without the analgesic effect of pain blocking (see PCP, FRY CIGARETTES, ILLY)

EMERALD TRIANGLE   The California counties of Mendocino, Humbolt, and Trinity. This area is know for growing the high grade Sinsemilla Marijuana

EQUIPMENT   Drug paraphernalia

E-PRESSED   Slang for the after effects of MDMA (Ecstasy) - depression due to the draining of serotonin levels by this drug

E PUDDLE   Refers to MDMA (Ecstasy) abusers as they often pile up together due to fatigue and/or the general effects of the drug; also called a Cuddle Puddle

EQUIPOISE   A veterinary steroid product, commonly diverted and abused by steroid users, that contains boldenone undecylenate

E-TARD   Someone on MDMA, Ecstasy

E-TARDATION   The "dumbing down" effects of abusing the drug MDMA

EUPHORIA or U4EUH   Hallucinogen 4-methylaminorex

EVERCLEAR   1) 190 proof grain alcohol; **2)** slang for gamma hydroxybutyrate (GHB)

EYE CANDY   Refers to flashing lights and toys that captivate people who are on the drug MDMA

EYE OPENER   The first Heroin injection of the day

FACTORY   A location where illicit drugs are produced for street sale

FANTASIA   Dimethyltryptamine or DMT

FANTASY   Gamma hydroxybutyrate (GHB) nickname common in Australia where is has been widely abused by bodybuilders and raver/club attendees

FENTANYL   A powerful anesthetic drug. Fentanyl may be diverted from hospitals for use. Analogs of fentanyl are usually manufactured illegally in clandestine drug labs

FINGER   An amount of Marijuana or Hashish

FIRE A LINE   To snort (inhale) an amount of a powdered drug

FIRE UP   To light and smoke a Cocaine or Methamphetamine pipe

FIRE WATER   A GBL product sold as a dietary supplement but now illegal as a GHB analog

FIRED UP   A drug high usually associated with Cocaine or Methamphetamine

FIT   Paraphernalia for injecting drugs

FIVE CENTS   Five dollars worth of a drug

FIX   To inject a drug

FLAKE   Cocaine

FLAKY   Acting crazy

FLASH/FLASHING   The first effect of a drug

FLASHBACK   A reoccurrence of a drug usually associated with L.S.D. or P.C.P. The drug is stored in the fat cells and may reenter the body months or even years after the last ingestion

FLASH POWDER   Methamphetamine

STREET SLANG GLOSSARY

FLATLINERS Street drug 4-methylthioamphetamine (4-MTA), also called Golden Eagle

FLIP Polydrug abuse referring to taking, or "flipping" MDMA with other drugs for variation of effects (See CANDY FLIP, HIPPIE FLIP, ELEPHANT FLIP, SEXTASY, LUCKY FLIP)

FLIP OUT To experience a severe psychological reaction to a drug

FLOATING Intoxicated

FLUFFING Chopping up Cocaine with a razor blade into a fine powder. It is then strained through mesh to increase its volume

FLYING SAUCER Trade name for Morning Glory seeds

FOILING Placing a drug, usually Heroin, on a piece of tin foil, then heating it up and inhaling the smoke

FOURS 60 mg. Codeine tablets stamped with the number 4

FOXY or FOXY METHOXY Street drug 5-methoxy-N,N-diisopropyltryptamine (5-MEO-DIPT), usually seen in pills with a spider or alien imprint

FREAK One who chronically uses large amounts of a specific drug

FREEBASE or FREEBASING A style of smoking rock cocaine

FREEZE **1)** Unavailability of drugs; **2)** Numbness caused by using cocaine

FRIED **1)** Drug high; **2)** Close to an overdose

FRONT **1)** To acquire drugs when payment is to be made by a reliable third party known to the seller; **2)** To purchase drugs on a short term credit

FRUIT SALAD A reckless combination of drugs

FRY CIGARETTES or FRY STICKS Regular cigarettes or marijuana cigarettes dipped in PCP and/or embalming fluid (See PCP, EMBALMING FLUID & WETS)

GANJA Hindu for Marijuana. Also used in the Jamaican culture

GAP To yawn (One of the earliest symptoms of heroin withdrawal)

GARBAGE Low grade drugs

GBL Gamma butyrolactone, primary ingredient for GHB and an active analog that turns rapidly into GHB in the human body. GBL is a degreasing solvent (See ANALOG)

GEE Gasket between needle and syringe

GEED UP or JEED UP or G'D UP High on gamma hydroxybutyrate (GHB)

GEEZE To inject a drug

GET DOWN   To use drugs, but is usually associated with Heroin

GET OFF   The first effects of a drug

GHB   Gamma hydroxybutyric acid (like liquid ecstasy). Illegal in U.S. except for limited prescription use under the tradename Xyrem (federal Schedule III drug). If Xyrem is diverted for abuse, it is treated as a Schedule I drug, the same as illicit GHB

GINA   Common gym name for gamma hydroxybutyrate (GHB)

GIRL   Cocaine

GLASS   Pure, solid, smokable form of Crystal Methamphetamine (See ICE)

GOD'S MEDICINE   Morphine

GO/GO FAST   Outdated term for stimulant drugs, usually associated with Amphetamines

GOLD   A particularly potent form of Marijuana grown in the Acapulco area (See ACAPULCO GOLD and GOLD LEAF)

GOLD DUST   Cocaine

GOLDEN CRESCENT   The Opium producing area of Southwest Asia (Iran, Pakistan, and Afghanistan)

GOLDEN TRIANGLE   The Opium producing area of Southeast Asia (Burma, Laos, and Thailand)

GOLD LEAF   A particularly potent form of Marijuana grown in the Acapulco area (See ACAPULCO GOLD and GOLD)

GOMA   Spanish word for Mexican Tar Heroin

GOODS   Refers to narcotics

GOOFBALLS   Barbiturates

GRAM   Common amount or measurement of a drug

GRASS   Marijuana

GRAVEL   Crack Cocaine

GRIFA   Spanish word for Marijuana

GUIDE   A baby sitter for an abuser of hallucinogenic drugs during an experience

GUN   Injection paraphernalia H Heroin

HABIT   Drug addiction

HALF   1/2 gram or 1/2 ounce of a drug

HALLUCINOGEN   Also referred to as psychedelic drugs, these substances may be either natural or synthetic and produce various intensities of hallucinations—perceptual changes involving sound, sight, sense of touch or smell, etc.

HAMMER COMING DOWN   The rapid and dramatic transition from a normal feeling state to that which results from a full impact of a drug. Usually in reference to the effects of a drug intravenously administered

HARD DRUGS   Narcotic analgesics. Also used to cover any drug which is controlled by a federal narcotic statutes, such as cannabis or cocaine

HANYAK   Solid, smokable Methamphetamine

HAPPY DRUG or HAPPY PILL   The drug MDMA

HAPPY DUST   Cocaine

HARD STUFF   Heroin

HASH   The isolated active ingredient of the Marijuana plant, THC; Hash comes in solid and oil form

HAY   Marijuana

HEAD   A heavy regular user of a drug. Reference is often made to a specific drug, such as "Acid Head"

HEAD SHOP   A store that sells drug paraphernalia and other related drug items

HEARTS   Dexedrine tablets

HEAVENLY BLUE   Strain of blue Morning Glory seeds which can be abused by sucking large quantities or making tea from them. Legend is that the blue ones are more potent.

HEAVES   Violent vomiting occurring during drug withdrawal

HEMP   Marijuana

HERB   Marijuana

HIERBA   Street name (Spanish) for marijuana

HIGH   Drug induced euphoria

HIPPIE or HIPPY FLIP   Polydrug flip of MDMA and magic mushrooms

HIT   **1)** Injection of drugs;**2)** A puff of a Marijuana Cigarette

HIT UP   **1)** To inject a drug;**2)** To borrow or attempt to borrow

HOG   P.C.P. (Phencyclidine)

HOLDING   To possess drugs

HONEY OIL   Purified Hashish Oil containing the highest concentration of THC

HOOKA   Marijuana smoking pipe or bong (See BONG)

HOOKED   Addicted to drugs

HORN   To snort (inhale) drugs in powder form

HORSE   Heroin

HOT SHOT   A very pure dose of Heroin which can result in death

HOUSEWIFE'S DISEASE   Dependence on tranquilizers

HUBBA   Cocaine Freebase

HUFFER A person who uses inhalants such as glue, paint thinner, petroleum products, etc

HUFFING The act of using inhalants

HUG DRUG MDMA (Ecstasy)

HUNTING Desperately seeking drugs prior to the onset of withdrawal

HUSTLING Addicts attempts to obtain enough money to purchase more drugs

HYPE Heroin addict

ICE Pure, solid, smokable form of Crystal Methamphetamine (See GLASS). Also refers to 4-methylaminorex, which is often called Euphoria or U4EUH.

ILLY CIGARETTE or ILLIES Regular cigarettes or marijuana cigarettes dipped in PCP and/or embalming fluid (See EMBALMING FLUID, WETS, FRYS)

J Marijuana

JAB To inject

JACKING OFF THE NEEDLE After putting the needle into the vein, some users pull the needle in and out of the wound to be sure the needle is still in the vein. This is usually associated with Heroin use

JAG State of being under influence of solvents

JANE Marijuana

JAR 100 or 1000 pills, also known as jug

JELLY Cocaine

JET FUEL P.C.P.

JIB Street name for gamma hydroxybutyrate (GHB)

JIM JONES Street gang term for Marijuana cigarette laced with Cocaine and dipped in P.C.P.

JIMSON WEED A hallucinogenic weed from the Datura genus (See DATURA)

JOINT Marijuana cigarette

JOLT The first effects of a drug

JONES A drug habit JOY POP Irregular use of narcotics

JONESING Needing a drug fix

JOY POPPING To inject just under the skin usually associated with Heroin use

JUG 1,000 pills

JUICE 1) Cheap wine; 2)More recently, liquid preparations of narcotic analgesic cough suppressants; 3) P.C.P. (Phencyclidine); 4) steroids; 5) GHB

JUNK Diluted Heroin

STREET SLANG GLOSSARY

JUNKIE Drug addict

JUNK WEED Low grade Marijuana

K Kilogram (2.2 pounds)

K or KET Ketamine

KAKSONJAE Pure, solid, smokable form of Crystal Methamphetamine

KAVA KAVA Sold as a dietary supplement, kava is a root common to the South Pacific, containing piper methysticum, that is a mild depressant

KETAMINE Animal tranquilizer for small animals, especially cats, that is also used on a limited basis in humans (in pediatrics and as a war zone anesthetic)

K-HOLE A ketamine induced out of body and/or comatose state

KIBBLES & BITS Street gang term for small pieces of freebase cocaine

KEG 50,000 pills

KEESTER PLANT Drugs which are hidden in the rectum

KGB (KILLER GREEN BUD) Marijuana

KHAT A plant common to areas like Somolia; leaves are chewed for stimulant effect of cathinone (when leaves are fresh) or cathine (once dried) (See CATHINONE and CATHINE)

KICK Stop using drugs

KILLER JOINT or KILLER WEED **1)** Marijuana cigarette laced with P.C.P.; **2)** Very potent Marijuana

KILO Kilogram (2.2 pounds)

KINGS HABIT The use of Cocaine

KIT Paraphernalia for injecting drugs

KITTY FLIP The polydrug abuse of using MDMA and ketamine together; abusers are advised to take the MDMA 15 minutes before taking the ketamine (See FLIP)

KJ P.C.P. saturated menthol cigarette (See KOOL JOINT)

KNOCKOUT DRUGS Liquid Chloral Hydrate or other drug, typically used with alcohol, to facilitate rape or robbery; NOTE: Despite the terminology, not all drugs used to facilitate rape result in being unconscious. Amnesia is the primary effect for many of them and unconsciousness may or may not occur at some point

KONA GOLD High grade Hawaiian Marijuana

KOOL JOINT Menthol cigarette laced with P.C.P. (See KJ)

KRYSTAL Crystal Methamphetamine

L L.S.D.

LACE To add a drug to another substance. Example: To spray P.C.P. on Marijuana for smoking

LACTONE Gammabutyrolactone (GBL), which is the primary ingredient in GHB but also an active analog; if consumed, GBL converts rapidly in the body to GHB

LADY Cocaine

LAUGHING GAS Nitrous oxide, used legitimately by dentists mixed with controlled level of oxygen but abused by huffing for the brief high that may result in brief unconsciousness (See NITROUS OXIDE)

L.A. TURNAROUNDS Amphetamines

L.B. 1 pound of a drug

LEAF Marijuana

LEAPERS Amphetamines

LEB Lebanese Hashish

LIBS The prescription drug Librium

LID An ounce of marijuana

LIGHT UP To smoke marijuana

LINE An amount of powdered drugs such as cocaine, meth, MDMA or ketamine that is combed (with a credit card or razor) into thin lines (on a mirror or glass or smooth surface) for snorting (with a straw or rolled up paper currency, etc.) (See BUMP)

LIQUID XTC or LIQUID X or LIQUID ECSTASY Refers to the drug GHB which is most commonly found in liquid state; does not refer to MDMA (Ecstasy) though some abusers have accidentally taken it believing it is a liquid version of MDMA

LOADED Under the influence of a drug

LOADS Tylenol w/ Codeine #4 and Doriden

LOCO WEED Marijuana

LOVE DRUGS MDA, Methqualone

LOVE FLIP Polydrug abuse of MDMA and Mescaline

LOVELY P.C.P.

L. S. A. d-lysergic acid amide is a precursor chemical to LSD and can be derived by sucking on morning glory seeds or drinking tea made from the seeds

L.S.D. The synthetic hallucinogen D-Lysergic Acid Diethylamide

LUCKY FLIP Polydrug abuse of MDMA and Lucky 7 (2-CT-7)

LUCKY 7 Street drug 2C-T-7, also called Triptasy, T7, 7-UP and Blue Mystic (See TRYPTAMINE)

LUDES Quaaludes (No longer manufactured)

M **1)** Marijuana;**2)** Morphine

M&M's MDMA (3,4-Methylenedioxyl-N-Methylamphetamine)

MAGIC DUST PCP

MAGIC MUSHROOM Refers to Psilocybin

MAKE A BUY Purchase drugs

MAINLINE To inject intravenously

MAN Drug dealer or drug connection

MANICURE The removal of unusable parts of the Marijuana plant such as stocks, stems, seeds, etc

MANNITOL Cutter for cocaine

MAPS The Multidisciplinary Association for Psychedelic Studies is a nonprofit group that promotes research of all psychedelic drugs and promotes legalization

MARKS Puncture wounds or holes left from needle injection

MARKED UP Displaying puncture wounds from needle injections

MARY JANE Marijuana

MATCHBOX 1/2 ounce of marijuana

MAUI WOWIE High grade Marijuana from Hawaii

MDA Mellow Drug of America. The synthetic hallucinogen drug 3,4-Methylenedioxyamphetamine

MDMA 3,4-Methylenedioxy-N-Methylamphetamine is a synthetic hallucinogen with stimulant qualities

MEQUIN Methaqualone

MERCK Pharmaceutical Cocaine

MERSH Low grade Marijuana

MESC Mescaline

METH Methamphetamine

METHADONE Methadone is most commonly known for use in heroin addiction treatment; it is also a pain medication being more widely prescribed, resulting in increased abuse and deaths

METHCATHINONE A street drug stimulant related to meth and often called CAT

METH HEAD User of methamphetamine

MEXICAN BROWN Mexican brown heroin

MEXICAN MUD Mexican Black Tar Heroin

MICKEY FINN The combination of the prescription drug Chloral Hydrate and Alcohol

MICRO DOTS L.S.D. on very small tablets MIERA Spanish word for Heroin

MIKE Microgram

MILK From milk sugar. Crystals of lactose frequently used in diluting Heroin

MIND-BLOWING Referring to a drug that produces extraordinarily powerful reaction. Usually a favorable experience

MINI BEANS Small Benzedrine tablets

MISS EMMA Morphine

MITSUBISHI MDMA pill with the Mitsubishi corporate logo imprinted; pill may be round, triangular or pentagon shaped; a very common logo

MJ Marijuana

MMDA 3-Methoxy-4, 5 Methylenedioxyamphetamine which is a psychedelic Amphetamine

MOLLY The drug TFMPP or 1-(3-Trifluoromethylphenyl) piperazine is referred to as Molly and is typically in capsule form; same clientele as MDMA and similar effects

MONKEY The state of being in withdrawal from Heroin MOTA Spanish word for Marijuana MOUTH HABIT Oral drug use

MPPP One of the numerous, so called "Designer Drugs" similar to MPTP. Gives Heroin-like effects and can be made to look like White Heroin

MPTP Made from MPPP and is another "Designer Drug" with effects like White Heroin

MSM Methyl sulfone or methylsulfoylmethane is a naturally occurring organic sulfur compound, sold as a dietary supplement; also used as a cutting agent for meth; extends quantity and gives a whiter product

MUD Mexican Black Tar Heroin

MULE A drug smuggler who actually carries the drugs

MUNCHIES Constant snacking associated with Marijuana intoxication

MUSCLING Injecting drugs into the muscle and is most commonly associated with steroids

NAIL Hypodermic needle

NARC 1) A narcotics officer; 2) An informer; 3) To inform on someone, "To narc someone off"

NEBBIES The prescription drug Nembutal

NEEDLE FREAK One who injects drugs into the vein or skin

NEEDLE MAN An addict

NEXUS The drug 2-(4-Bromo-2,5-dimethoxy-phenyl)-ethylamine, also called 2C-B or Bromo

NEXUS FLIPPING Taking MDMA and Nexus (See FLIP)

NICKEL Five dollars

STREET SLANG GLOSSARY

NICKEL BAG   Five dollars worth of a drug

NINETEEN   A term for speed. The nineteenth letter of the alphabet is "S"

NOD   Being under the influence of Heroin. A relaxed state similar to sleep

NOSE CANDY   Cocaine

NOX   Abusing nitrous oxide while on MDMA

N2O (aka: NOZ)   Nitrous oxide, abused by inhaling, causing a very brief high and possible brief unconsciousness; not scheduled but some states have laws against possession with intent to inhale (gas, devices for inhaling, etc.) and for inhaling or being impaired to drive

NUBAIN   Brand name for the drug nalbuphine, an analgesic for moderate to severe pain; widely used by athletes, often resulting in abuse and addiction

NUKING THE COKE   During the Cocaine Freebasing process the Cocaine Hydrochloride is mixed with baking soda and water, then heated. The microwave is used to speed up the process. A coffee maker machine may also be used

NUTMEG   Cooking herb abused by some in high quantities (5-20 grams) for hallucinogenic effects; contains myristicin (also contained in mace)

O   **1)** Cocaine;**2)** Opium

O.D.   Overdose, usually a very serious condition

OIL   **1)** Hashish in oil form;**2)** Methamphetamine in oil form

OLLA   Cocaine

ONE HITTER   A drug that can only be diluted one time

ONE & ONE   Two lines of Cocaine, one for each nostril

ON THE PIPE   Street gang term for being addicted to Freebase Cocaine

ORANGE CRUSH   When the red pills of Coridicin Cough & Cold medication are crushed it results in an orange powder that is then snorted for the high from the DXM it contains (See DXM or DEXTROMETHORPHAN)

OTC   Over the counter. Refers to drugs that can be bought without a prescription

OUTFIT   Paraphernalia for injecting drugs

OUT OF SIGHT   **1)** Extraordinary quality, wonderful;**2)** A fantastic experience

OVERAMPED   An overdose usually associated with a stimulant drug (Cocaine or Methamphetamine)

OXY/OXYCOTTON OxyContin, brandname for the synthetic opiate oxycodone; widely abused for its powerful euphoria but also potentially deadly

OZ/OZER One ounce

PAKALOLO Hawaiian for Marijuana

PANAMA GOLD High grade Panamanian Marijuana

PANAMA RED High grade Panamanian Marijuana that has a red color to the leaves and a red fuzz on the under portion of the leaves

PANIC 1) An acute state of fear precipitated by the onset of withdrawl and frantic action to acquire drugs;**2)** An abrupt drying up of heroin sources, affecting all local addicts

PAPERS 1) Marijuana rolling papers (Zig-Zag being the most common);**2)** Blotter acid;**3)** A piece of paper folded like an envelope containing a small amount of a drug (See BINDLE)

PAPER ACID L.S.D.

PARACHUTE MDMA powder or crushed MDMA pills or coke powder may be wrapped in tissue and swallowed in the belief that letting the drug "parachute" down in that manner intensifies the effect

PARTY BOWL/PARTY BONG A Marijuana pipe (See BONG)

PAREST Methaqualone

PASTA/PASTE Raw coca extracted from the coca leaves to be refined into Cocaine Hydrochloride. The raw coca is often smoked by the local peasants because of its availability and inexpensive price

PAYS & OWES Paperwork (may be elaborate bookkeeping or scraps of paper) showing buyers, sales and/or money amounts re drug distribution; may be in code

P.C.P. Phencyclidine

P.D.R. Physician's Desk Reference. A book that contains all the pharmaceutical drugs. Used by doctors

P.C.E. N-Ethyl-1 -Phenycyclhexylamine. An analog or member of the P.C.P. family of drugs

PEACE WEED Marijuana laced with P.C.P.

PEAKING Reaching the highest point while under the influence of a drug

PEARL Cocaine

PEARLS Amyl Nitrite

PEANUT BUTTER CRANK Low grade crude Methamphetamine

PEDAZO Spanish word for Heroin

PEP PILL Amphetamine

PERCS   The prescription drug Percodan

PERICO   Spanish word for Cocaine

PERSIAN BROWN   Raw, unprocessed Morphine sold on the streets as Heroin

PERSIAN WHITE   High grade Persian Heroin

PERUVIAN FLAKE   South American high grade Cocaine and refers to the shape of the Cocaine crystals

PEYOTL   American Indian name for the Peyote Cactus

PEZ   LSD-laced PEZ candies

PHARMING   The dangerous practice of mixing a variety of prescription and/or over-the-counter medications in a bowl at a party and grabbing a few without regard for dosage and drug interaction; also called TRAIL MIX

PHENETHYLAMINES   A class of chemical compounds that produce hallucinogenic effects and varying degrees of stimulation, best known being MDMA, MDA, MDEA, 2-CB

PHENNIES   The prescription drug Phenobarbital

PIECE   1 ounce, or 1 pound, of a drug

PILL FREAK   User of any type of pills

PILLOW   **1)** Methamphetamine;**2)** Package of 1,000 Amphetamine tablets;**3)** Methaqualone

PINNED   Constricted pupils (the size of a pinhead) that result when under the influence of Heroin or other narcotics

PIN/PINNER   A very thin Marijuana cigarette

PINK HEARTS   **1)** Prescription drug Preludin;**2)** Fake stimulants that can be ordered out of magazines and contain Caffeine and/or Ephedrine

PINK LADIES   The prescription drug Darvon

PINKS   Seconal (named for the color of the capsule)

PIPERAZINE   A veterinary animal wormer; variations of it are abused drugs (See BZP and TFMPP) with stimulant and somewhat MDMA-like properties

PIPERIDINE   Used to make PCP

PLATEAUING   Peaking out on a drug to the point where the user no longer feels the designated effects. Usually used to describe steroids

PLUGGING   The practice of rectal insertion of MDMA pills

PLUR   Raver term standing for Peace Love Unity and Respect

POLVO   Spanish word for Cocaine

POP   **1)** To take a tablet orally;**2)** To inject subcutaneous

POPPERS Amyl and Butyl Nitrite, which is administered by crushing the small vile in which it is contained and immediately inhaling the vapors

POPPING 1) To swallow a drug; **2)** To inject a drug under the skin, not directly into the vein

POT Marijuana

POT HEAD Marijuana user

POWDERED Under the influence of Cocaine

P-2-P Phenyl-2-Propanone. A chemical used to make methamphetamine

PRIMO Street gang term for a Marijuana cigarette laced with Cocaine

PROCAINE Adulterant used to dilute the strength of cocaine or Mexican brown heroin. Has pharmacological action of its own

PROP Phenly-2-Propanone. A chemical used for manufacturing Methamphetamine

PSYCHEDELIC A drug that distorts visual, auditory, and tactile senses

PUNTA ROJA High grade Columbium Marijuana

PURPLE HEARTS Phenobarbital (Luminal tablets)

PURPLE STICKY Brand name in head shops for Mexican salvia (See SALVIA DIVINORUM)

PUSHER Seller of drugs at the street level Q'S Methaqualone

PYRAMIDS Brightly colored gelatin LSD on pieces of diffuser plastic (from fluorescent light fixtures, for example); may be pealed off of the plastic and cut into little strips like modern-day breath mint strips or the plastic may be perforated and then broken into square or rectangular pieces which are sucked on by the user

QUARTER 1) 1/4 gram of a drug; **2)** 1/4 ounce of a drug; **3)** $25.00 worth of a drug

QUARTER PIECE 1/4 ounce of a certain drug RACK 2-5 capsules wrapped in tin foil

RAGWEED Low grade Marijuana

RAILS Lines of a powdered drug laid beside each other, on a mirror or a piece of glass, in preparation for snorting (inhaling)

RAINBOWS Tuinal® (a combination of amobarbital and secobarbital) so called because of the bright red and blue capsules (see Red & Blues)

RAT An informer

RAVE PARTY All night electronic music party where most attendees use hallucinogens, especially MDMA (Ecstasy), and other drugs

REDS/REDEVILS 1) Seconal; 2) also refers to the red tablets containing DXM marketed as Coricidin Cough and Cold (See also ROBOTRIPPIN' and DXM)

RED & BLUES Tuinal. Bright red and blue capsules (see Rainbows)

REEFER A Marijuana cigarette

REGISTER To find the vein when injecting

RENEWTRIENENT A common GHB analog product disguised as a dietary supplement but illegal for human consumption; usually contains GBL

RESIN The active ingredient of the Marijuana plant. THC (Delta-9-Tetrahydrocannabinol)

RIB Flunitrazepam, also known as Rohypnol

RICIN A poisonous natural extract isolated from castor beans; falsely claimed to be used by meth traffickers to kill police officers, as per a fake alert that was being distributed via email in recent years (For info on false email, see SNOPES)

RIG The paraphernalia used to inject drugs

RIPPED 1) Exhausted after a several day amphetamine run; 2) adversely affected by a drug; 3) very muscular and lean

RIPPERS Amphetamines

RIPPED OFF 1) Robbed; 2) Cheated in a drug buy

ROACH The butt end of a Marijuana cigarette

ROACH CLIP Any object used to hold the last bit of a burning Marijuana cigarette. An electrical alligator clip or surgical hemostat are commonly used

ROACHED OUT High on flunitrazepam, tradename Rohypnol

ROBOTRIPPIN' On DXM, named for Robitussin products that contain dextromethorphan, a cough suppressant that causes hallucinations in high doses

ROCA Spanish word for Crack

ROCK Freebased Cocaine Hydrochloride

ROCK UP The process of converting Cocaine Hydrochloride to Cocaine base

ROCKET FUEL P.C.P.

ROIDS General term for steroids

ROID RAGE The uncontrollable, violent temperament displayed by some steroid users

ROLL 10 pills sold in tin foil

ROLLS MDMA pills

ROLLING or ROLLIN' On MDMA (Ecstasy)

ROLLER PAPERS Cigarette rolling papers used to make Marijuana cigarettes

ROMPUM Horse or large animal tranquilizer, analgesic, and muscle relaxant Xylazine; limited abuse by humans reported for euphoric effect

ROOFIES/ROOPIES Flunitrazepam, tradename Rohypnol

ROPE Marijuana

RUBBY A skid row alcoholic who on occasion resorts to propyl (rubbing) alcohol

RUDERALIS Russian Marijuana plant. It has a low percentage of THC, the active ingredient in Marijuana

RUFFIES Flunitrazepam, tradename Rohypnol

RUMMY Skid row alcoholic

RUN A period of several consecutive days during which an individual uses Methamphetamines several times a day with little food or sleep

RUNNER Drug smuggler or transporter

RUSH An intense sensation which rapidly follows intravenous administration of such drugs as heroin, amphetamines or cocaine

SAFROLE Key ingredient in MDMA; may appear as iso-safrole, bromo-safrole or chloro-safrole; a sassafras extract but is not present in sassafras candies sold legitimately. No legitimate chemical use in the USA

SALTY WATER Nickname for GHB. Also referred to as WATER

SALVIA DIVINORUM A hallucinogenic plant from the mint family that grows wild in some regions of Mexico and used by shamans there; active ingredient is salvinorin A, not scheduled as of 2005. More powerful than marijuana. Being touted on the Internet and in head shops (See PURPLE STICKY)

SATIVA Marijuana. Comes from the scientific name Cannabis Sativa

SCHOOL BOY Codeine, so called because of the mildness of its effects when compared with the more potent narcotic analgesics

SCOOP Common nickname for the drug GHB

SCOPOLAMINE One of the alkaloids in Datura plants, legitimately used as a motion sickness medication and in pre-surgery to induce amnesia; also used as a rape drug

SCORE To make a successful drug purchase

SCRATCH Money

SCREENS Round metal mesh screens placed in a smoking pipe to hold the drug in the bowl

SCRIBE A person who writes false prescriptions

SCRIPT Drug prescription

SCRIPT WRITER Physician willing to write prescriptions for drugs

SECOS Seconal

SEND IT HOME To inject narcotic analgesics, cocaine or amphetamines intravenously

SERVE Street gang term for selling drugs

SES Sinsemilla Marijuana (Sinsemilla means without seeds)

SET A combination of the prescription drugs Doriden and Tylenol w/Codeine #4

SET UP A situation in which undercover police officers entice a person to sell them drugs for the purpose of bringing about the person's arrest

SEXTASY The "flip" of taking MDMA and Viagra together. The Viagra helps overcome the erectile dysfunction or blockage of orgasms that MDMA may cause

SHABU Hawaiian word for the smokable form of Crystal Methamphetamine (See GLASS and ICE)

SHAKE The manicured leaves of a Marijuana plant

SHAVE 1) To adulterate, dilute or shortweight a drug; 2) Literally shave off minute quantities and thereby shortweight the buyer

SHEET ACID L.S.D. on blotter paper (See BLOTTER ACID)

SHERMS A heavy-stock dark brown paper cigarette that is dipped into P.C.P. and then smoked (Short for Shermans)

SHIT Low quality drugs usually refers to Heroin

SHOOT-UP To inject intravenously

SHOOTING GALLERY A place where heroin addicts congregate to inject

SHORTCHANGED Having been sold drugs which are usually inferior in quality or purity

SHOTGUNNING Using any available steroid

SHOT IN THE ARM Although the general use of the term is now broader, it originally referred to an injection of narcotics, which is followed by a state of peacefulness, reverie and well-being

SHROOMS The hallucinogenic Psilocybin Mushrooms

SICKNESS The onset of withdrawal

SINSEMILLA Spanish for "without seed." Marijuana from unfertilized female plants; it is a method of growing, not a variety of marijuana

SIPPIN' SYRUP Drinking codeine cough syrup (promoted in a rap song)

SKAG Heroin

SKIN POPPING Injecting subcutaneous

SKITTLES or SKITTLING Refers to being on DXM (See DEXTROMETHORPHAN)

SKUNK WEED High grade Marijuana with a strong odor

SLAB A large, flat piece of Freebased cocaine

SLAMMING To inject. Usually refers to Heroin use

SLEEPERS Sedative/hypnotic drugs such as barbiturates

SLOW AND LOW Heroin users, when under the influence are said to be slow and low, in that they move slowly and speak in a low slow, slurred voice

SMACK Heroin

SMART DRINK Liquid concoctions containing various amino acids said to increase the intelligence of the user. Common at "rave" parties

SMASHED Heavily intoxicated with alcohol or other drugs

SMOKE Marijuana

SMOKE HOUSE A structure where users go to smoke Freebase Cocaine. They "rent" the pipes which contain the drug and leave the pipe behind

SMURFS Blue MDMA pills, the color of Smurf cartoon characters

SNAPPERS Amyl or Butyl Nitrate SNAPS Street gang term for money

SNIFF 1) To take cocaine, amphetamines or heroin by inhaling through the nose;2) To inhale solvents through both the nose and mouth

SNOPES.COM One of several websites that provide info on email scams, fake emails, urban legends that get distributed widely is www.snopes.com. Good place to check out unusual email before sending it on to others and possibly perpetuating misinformation

SNORT To inhale a drug in powdered form. Usually refers to Cocaine

SNOT Black Tar Heroin

SNOW Cocaine

SNOW BIRD Cocaine

SNOW FLAKE Cocaine

SNOW BUGS   The sensation of bugs crawling on or under the skin of a Cocaine user

SNOW SEAL   A brand of non-porous smooth paper used to make bindles to carry drugs. Logo is a seal balancing a snowflake on its nose

SOAP   GHB

SOAPER/SOAP   Sopor (Methaqualone)

SODIUM OXYBATE   The drug GHB, tradename Xyrem

SOFT DRUGS   Drugs of abuse other than narcotics also applied to those drugs perceived to have low toxicity and/or dependency liability

SOLES   Slabs of solid Hashish

SOMA   Common street name and a tradename of the abused skeletal muscle relaxant carisoprodol, a depressant

SOURCE   A drug dealer or drug supplier

SPACE BASING   Freebased Cocaine dipped in P.C.P. and then smoked

SPACED   Unresponsive to the external environment, usually in reaction to altered consciousness produced by hallucinogenic drugs

SPACEY   Referring to a strangeness or a state of psychic deterioration produced by excessive and/or heavy, chronic use of drugs

SPEAKER TWEAKER   People high on MDMA who hang onto the speakers at raves for the intense sensation of sound and vibration

SPECIAL K   The drug ketamine

SPEED   Injectable methamphetamine

SPEEDBALL   Heroin plus cocaine

SPEEDFREAK   Heavy regular use of injectable methamphetamine

SPEED LAB   Laboratory where Methamphetamines are manufactured

SPEEDER   Methamphetamine user

SPIKE   Hypodermic needle

SPOON   **1)** Small metal spoon used to snort (inhale) drugs in powdered form;**2)** Teaspoon used to heat drugs prior to injection;**3)** Street measurement of a drug, usually an amount for personal use and usually refers to Heroin

SPORE   The reproductive part of the mushroom

SPORTING   Cocaine use

STACKING   The use of two or more steroids. One right after another, but not at the same time

STAR DUST   Cocaine

STASH   **1)** A place where drugs are hidden to escape detection in the event of a sudden search by authorities;**2)** To hide drugs rapidly when confronted with a search

STASH CANS   Common brand name items, such as beer cans, motor oil cans, in which the bottom or top screws off and the drugs are hidden inside

STEP-ON   To dilute a drug

STICK   A Marijuana cigarette

STINK WEED   Low grade Marijuana

STONED   Pleasurably intoxicated

STOOLIE   An informant

S.T.P.   Serenity, Tranquility, Peace. The synthetic hallucinogen 2,5-Dimethoxy-4-Methlyamphetamine

STRAWBERRY   Street gang term for a female who exchanges sex for drugs

STRUNG OUT   **1)** In an emaciated and generally poor state of health and appearance due to chronic drug use; 2) Heavily dependent on drugs;**3)** Sometimes to produce an extreme negative psychic effect during a single drug episode

STUFF   General term for drugs, specifically Heroin

SUGAR (MILK) HABIT   Addict's desire for sweets due to heavy amount of milk mixed with everyday heroin

SUNSHINE   L.S.D.

SUPER GRASS   **1)** P.C.P. laced Marijuana;**2)** High grade potent Marijuana

SUPER JOINT   Marijuana cigarette dipped in P.C.P.

SUPER K   The prescription drug Ketamine

SUPER WEED   **1)** High grade Marijuana;**2)** Marijuana laced with P.C.P.

SUPPLIER   Drug dealer or drug source

SWEAT IT OUT   To withdraw from narcotic analgesics

SWEEPING   Snorting (inhaling) drugs in powdered form

SWING MAN   A drug supplier

SWIRL or SWIRLING   The drug GHB; the sensation of being on GHB

T   The prescription drug Talwin

T'S AND BLUES   Pentazocine (Talwin) plus tripelennamine prepared in a solution and injected

TABS   L.S.D.

TAKE-OFF   The first effects of a drug

TAR   Mexican Black Tar Heroin

TASTE Sampling a drug before buying it

TATTOOING Prior to injecting, some users burn the end of the needle for sterilization. If the carbon deposits that form are not cleaned off prior to injecting, they will form under the skin causing dark marks. Same principle as a standard tattoo

TEA Marijuana

TEABAGGING Rectal insertion of tampon soaked in GHB

TEMPLE BALLS Hashish mixed with Opium then shaped into a small, round ball. Common in Nepal and parts of India

TEN CENTS Ten dollars

TEN CENT BAG Ten dollars worth of a drug

TFMPP The drug TFMPP or 1-(3-Trifluoromethylphenyl) piperazine is referred to as Molly and is typically in capsule form; same clientele as MDMA and similar effects (See MOLLY; also see BZP)

THAI STICK Potent Marijuana from Thailand whose buds are attached to six inch sticks with string

THC Delta 9-Tetrahydrocannabinol. The active ingredient of the Marijuana plant

THE MATRIX The cough suppressant DXM, referring to the red pill of Coricidin Cough & Cold and the movie by that name wherein a red pill is taken to enter the matrix

THRUSTERS Amphetamines

TIE A tourniquet tied around the arm to inhibit blood flow so the vein will bulge for injecting. Example: Belt, scarf, hose, surgical tubing, etc

TIE UP To apply a belt or tourniquet to the arm or leg to produce distention of a vein for an injection

TIE RAG (See TIE)

TIME FLIP The flip of MDMA and DMT (See FLIP and DMT)

T.M.A. Trimethoxyamphetamine. Similar to M.D.A.

TOKE 1) A puff of a marijuana cigarette; 2) To take a puff

TOKER Marijuana smoker

TOOLS Drug paraphernalia

TOOT Cocaine

TOOTER A piece of a drinking straw, a rolled up dollar bill, or other device used for snorting (inhaling) powdered drugs

TOPS The top buds of the Marijuana plant rich in THC

TOTALED Exhausted after an acute drug experience

TRACKS, TRACK MARKS 1) Collapsed veins resulting from chronic injection; 2) discoloration and scars, resembling a tattoo in appearance, resulting from chronic injection

TRAIL MIX   Abuse of multiple prescription drugs and/or over the counter products (See PHARMING)

TRANK   P.C.P.

TRAVELER   A user of hallucinogenic drugs

TREATMENT   A dose of Heroin, especially when feeling the effects of withdrawal

TRIP   Under the influence of a drug. Usually refers to L.S.D.

TRIPPERS   L.S.D.

TRIPLE C   Dextromethorphan (See CCC and DXM)

TRIPLE STACK   An Ecstasy pill three times the normal thickness and dosage

TRYPTAMINES   Class of chemical compounds that produce hallucinogenic effects, most notorious being psilocybin mushrooms, DMT, 2C-T-7, AMT and FOXY

TUIES   The prescription drug Tuinal

TURN ON   **1)** To produce a state of pleasurable excitement (the stimulus may be either a drug or other experience);**2)** To introduce someone to a drug or drugs

TWEAKED   Under the influence of Methamphetamine sometimes refers to an adverse reaction

TWEAKER   Chronic meth abuser at the end of a binge period; dangerous time for confrontation with law enforcement due to high propensity for violence at this stage

UNCUT   A drug that has not been diluted

UP FRONT   **1)** As a sample, a small quantity of a drug is provided to the buyer to indicate quality;**2)** As proof, showing the seller the money before the drugs are produced

UPPERS   A general term used for most stimulant drugs of abuse, such as amphetamines, and related drugs. However, the term is not used for cocaine

UP TIGHT   Tense, nervous or frightened because of a subjective experience produced by either a drug or by real events

URINE METH   Saving urine from chronic users to process for the unmetabolized meth

USER   Someone who uses drugs or is an addict U.S.P. Pharmaceutical Methamphetamine

VALS   The prescription drug Valium

VAPORS   Gang term for Freebase Cocaine smoke

VEGETABLE   One who suffers from severe brain or behavioral impairment to the point of being unable to care for oneself

VITAMIN K   The drug ketamine (See SPECIAL K)

WACK   **1)** To dilute or cut a drug;**2)** P.C.P.

STREET SLANG GLOSSARY

WAFER COCAINE Rock cocaine in appearance of wafers or pasta style (instead of the typical "rock" format), classic of 18th Street Gang

WAKE-UPS Amphetamines

WASHBACK A method used to get any usable drug out of a pipe after it has been used several times (See WASHBACK METHODS)

WASTED Exhausted after an acute drug experience, usually in reference to amphetamines or cocaine

WATER 1) Methamphetamine; 2) GHB

WATER PIPE A smoking pipe that has a chamber that is filled with water or wine. The chamber is used to cool the smoke (See BONG)

WEDGES Flat L.S.D. tablets

WEED 1) Marijuana; 2) Tobacco

WEEKENDER An occasional drug user

WET DADDIES P.C.P.

WETS Marijuana cigarettes dipped in PCP and/or embalming fluid (See FRYS, PCP, EMBALMING FLUID, ILLY)

WHIP-ITS or WHIPPITS or WHIPPETS Small nitrous oxide canisters, slightly smaller than CO2 cartridges, used to power whipped cream makers and often abused by inhalation (See CRACKERS, NITROUS OXIDE, N2O)

WHITE 1) Cocaine; 2) Asian Heroin

WHITE GIRL Cocaine

WHITES Amphetamine tablets

WHITE STUFF Heroin, usually Chinese

WIGGIN or WIGGING 1) Bizarre behavior on mind-altering drugs; 2) in need of drugs; 3) on MDMA (Ecstasy)

WINDOW PANE L.S.D. that is placed on small squares of gelatin

WIPED OUT To have lost consciousness from abusing drugs

WIRED 1) Chronically dependent on amphetamines; 2) Physically dependent on heroin

WIRED-OUT High on Cocaine or Methamphetamine

WITHDRAW The effects of quitting the heavy use of narcotics

WORKS Paraphernalia for injecting drugs

WRECKED 1) Exhausted after an acute drug experience; 2) Having a very bad drug experience

X M.D.M.A.-(3,4-Methylenedioxly-N-Mtheylamphetamine)

XTC Also known as Ecstacy, MDMA, and Adam. Psychedelic drug common to "rave" parties

YABA Also called the CRAZY DRUG, YABA is simply pills of meth or a combo of meth/ephedrine; designed to market to teens with the pill format, colors and logos, similar to MDMA marketing

YELLOWS, YELLOW JACKETS Nembutal (Pentobarbital sodium)

YEN Agitated sleep occurring during withdrawal from heroin Z One ounce of a drug

ZANY BARS The drug alprazolam, tradename Xanax, a benzodiazepine depressant; refers to the format sometimes used for this drug which is bars with marks for breaking off doses as directed

ZIP/ZIPPY Amphetamines

ZONKED Extremely high on drugs

This page intentionally left blank.

Index

Index